# Gawdawful Hymns

## A Collection of Parodies of Christian Hymns, and More...

Ward Ricker

First Edition Design Publishing
Sarasota, Florida USA

Gawdawful Hymns
Copyright ©2018  Ward Ricker

ISBN 978-1506-906-42-3 PRINT
ISBN 978-1506-906-43-0 EBOOK

LCCN 2018947899

June 2018

Published and Distributed by
First Edition Design Publishing, Inc.
P.O. Box 20217, Sarasota, FL 34276-3217
www.firsteditiondesignpublishing.com


ALL RIGHTS RESERVED. No part of this book publication may be reproduced, stored in a retrieval system, or transmitted in any form or by any means — electronic, mechanical, photo-copy, recording, or any other — except brief quotation in reviews, without the prior permission of the author or publisher.

Cover Art - Amber Espeland

Author can be contacted through www.WardRicker.com

# WARNING:

The songs contained herein contain large amounts of truth, and may be be disturbing to or endanger the illusions of those holding to myth and superstition.
**Singer discretion is advised.**

*******

### ADDITIONAL ADVISORY:

These songs also contain ideas and language that may be offensive to some people, especially to those who hold serious beliefs in Christianity. This book is for enjoyment. If you are a serious Christian it is safe to say you won't enjoy it, so don't read it. If you do and are offended, it's your own damn fault. You have been warned!

To all those who have struggled to free themselves from myth and superstition.

# TABLE OF CONTENTS

Introduction .................................................................................. i
Part 1: Songs for Everyone .......................................................... 1
Part 2: Songs for Most Everyone ................................................ 19
Part 3: Songs for Some ............................................................... 41
Part 4: Songs for a Few ............................................................... 81
Part 5: Songs for Hardcore Atheists .......................................... 117
Part 6: Christmas Non-Carols .................................................... 127
Part 7: Original Music by Author .............................................. 137
Index .......................................................................................... 171

# INTRODUCTION

This book contains hymns that I rewrote, mostly over the course of 2017, although a few of the songs I had written previously. I refer to them as parodies, because, in general, I am trying to use humor to poke fun at religious themes. However, parody may not be a proper description for all the songs herein. Some are not humorous, and some have nothing whatsoever to do with the original message of the hymn or even with Christianity or religion at all. I have peace songs, songs about hiking, kayaking and tennis, and even songs about eating. However, the main theme of this songbook is a humorous critique of Christianity, so I am referring to this as a book of parodies. (Any non-parody songs are covered by the "and More..." part of the subtitle.)

Whereas these songs are generally poking fun at religious ideas, sometimes in rather strong manner, many of them may be offensive to many Christians. But that's okay. I doubt that anyone would care if I wrote songs that made fun of Zeus, Thor or the sun god Ra. Ideas about god and Jesus are just as superstitious and preposterous as those are. So, fair game! If you find such humor offensive, then please feel free to not read or sing them. For the rest of you, I hope that you get as much pleasure out of reading or singing them as I did in writing them.

Attribution to the writers of the original hymns has been made as well as possible. Sources do not always agree. When they haven't, I have made my best guess. In a few cases where I have no idea what to make of confusing or conflicting information I have just inserted question marks.

As parodies, I try to keep some of the original words of the hymn and change some of the words. The songs range from very few words changes, such as "I'll Troll Where You Want Me to Troll", to those in which I have thrown the entire text away and completely written my own lyrics, such as "Job, He Is My Man", (and therefore is probably not truly a parody). In some cases (*e.g.*, "Sunshine on My Pole") I have suckered you in by using the first verse exactly as originally written, then "unsuspectingly" changed words in following stanzas.

The songs or "hymns" are arranged in seven sections. The first five sections are in increasing order of "inclusiveness", that is, how broad of an audience they would likely appeal to (or, if you prefer, how outraged a Christian would be to read or hear the songs in that section). The first section contains songs that should be appropriate for anyone, that is, that probably no one will object to (or, if you prefer, would not likely outrage any Christians). Basically, these are songs which say nothing about Christianity or religion. The fifth section contains songs that would probably only be "appropriate" for die-hard atheists (ie, will probably outrage everyone who calls him- or herself a Christian). Of course, these are my own judgments. You may draw your own conclusions about how appropriately the songs are categorized. The sixth section contains Christmas carols that I have rewritten in similar manner. (A couple of these are taken from secular Christmas songs "The Twelve Days of Christmas" and "Deck the Halls", which probably cannot truly be called hymns.) The seventh section contains songs that I have written to my own original music. These last two sections are organized without re-gard to "appropriateness of audience."

The songs in this volume range from the serious ("Stand Up For Peace" to the uproarious ("The First 'Oh, Hell!'"), from the logical ("His Eye Is on the Sparrow") to the ridiculous ("There Shall Be Plowers Undressing"), from those that have a real message about religion ("Onward Christian Soldiers") to those that are just foolish ("Jesus Shaves") or even gross ("Love Divine, Your Butt Is Smelling").

If I changed the name of the hymn the original name appears underneath the name I gave it. If no name appears underneath, then the name is the same as the original hymn. Some tunes are used more than once.

Some songs are written from a "male perspective". Ladies can decide whether they wish to sing them or not. There is also one song that the men can decide if they wish to sing or not.

All the hymns that were used in this work were published prior to 1923 and are therefore in the public domain. To my knowledge it is perfectly legal to publish parodies of songs or any other works that are still under copyright, but since some songs may not be considered "true" parodies, I am using only those hymns old enough to be in the public domain.

There are a total of 276 rewritten hymns, plus 30 songs written to my own music.

If anyone is interested on my more serious thoughts on religious topics, or any other topics, you may have access to my website:www.wardricker.com.

Enjoy!

Ward Ricker, Author

# Part 1

## Songs for Everyone

These are songs you can share freely with all your Christian friends.

## Eat Your Squash and Your Spuds
(Tune: Are You Washed In the Blood?)

Are you having lamb in your chow tonight?
Eat your squash and your spuds with your lamb.
Include some vegetables in every bite.
Eat your squash and your spuds with your lamb.

Are you eating too heavily of meat in your meals?
Eat your squash and your spuds with your lamb.
Then eat more veggies, see how good it feels!
Eat your squash and your spuds with your lamb.

Oh yes, lamb is delicious as a kind of meat,
Eat your squash and your spuds with your lamb.
But vegetables are very important to eat.
Eat your squash and your spuds with your lamb.

Oh yes, eating those vegetables good health will bring,
Eat your squash and your spuds with your lamb.
So that with energy these songs you can sing.
Eat your squash and your spuds with your lamb.

CHORUS:
Eat your squash and your spuds.
Eat your squash and your spuds with your lamb.
A well-balanced diet is important to have.
Eat your squash and your spuds with your lamb.

Original Words: Elisha A. Hoffman, 1878

## Broccoli and Tender Peas
(Tune: Softly and Tenderly)

Broccoli and tender peas Jesus is serving, serving to you and to me.
Some good nutrition you're surely deserving you'll get in each broccoli or pea.

Broccoli and tender peas Jesus will feed you, so come on now and enjoy.
Eat lots of green veggies. You really need to, to be a strong girl or strong boy.

Broccoli and tender peas Jesus says eat them. They're good for body and mind.
Healthy green vegetables, you cannot beat them. What great nutrition you'll
    find.

CHORUS:
Come eat. Come eat. Ye who are hungry come eat.
Broccoli and tender peas Jesus is serving. If you want good health then come eat.

Original Words: Will L. Thompson, 1880

## Oily Peas for Christ
(Tune: Loyalty to Christ)

From over hill and plain there comes the signal strain
Of oily peas, oily peas, oily peas for Christ.
Its music rolls along. The hills take up the song.
Of oily peas, oily peas, yes oily peas for Christ.

Oh, hear, ye brave, the sound that moves the earth around,
Of oily peas, oily peas, oily peas for Christ.
Arise and dare to do. Oh, pick peas not a few.
Oh, oily peas, oily peas, yes oily peas for Christ.

Come, join our loyal throng as we sing our glad song
Of oily peas, oily peas, oily peas for Christ.
Where Satan's beans once grew we'll plant peas not a few.
Oh, oily peas, oily peas, yes oily peas for Christ.

The strength of youth employ, oh, every girl and boy,
For oily peas, oily peas, oily peas for Christ.
Oh, lots of peas we'll grow, then oil them 'til they glow.
Oh, oily peas, oily peas, yes oily peas for Christ.

CHORUS:
"On to victory! On to pick the peas!"
Cries our great commander, "On!"
We'll move at his command, pick peas with every hand
For oily peas, oily peas, yes, oily peas for Christ.

Original Words: Elijah T. Cassel

## My Cheeses, I Love Thee
(Tune: My Jesus, I Love Thee)

My cheeses, I love thee -- a pleasure of mine.
For thee all the follies of Spam I resign.
Oh, parmesan and cheddar, my favorites art thou.
If ever I loved thee, my cheeses, 'tis now.

My cheeses, I love thee, an endless delight.
They cheer me and help me feel ever so bright.
On Gouda and Colby Jack I just love to chow.
If ever I loved thee, my cheeses, 'tis now.

My cheeses, I love thee. I'll love thee in death.
That Swiss and mozzarella I'll eat with my last breath.
Any cheese made from the milk of a goat or cow,
If ever I loved thee, my cheeses, 'tis now.

Original Words: William R. Featherstone, 1864

## There Is Flour in the Bread
(Tune: There Is Power in the Blood)

Would you o'er sickness a victory win?
There's flour in the bread, flour in the bread.
Would you live healthy and strong to the end?
There's wonderful flour in the bread.

Would you play hard and go run for great length?
There's flour in the bread, flour in the bread.
Eat some today so you'll build up your strength.
There's wonderful flour in the bread.

Would you be strong and have senses so keen?
There's flour in the bread, flour in the bread.
Have a slice now and you'll see what I mean.
There's wonderful flour in the bread.

Would you develop a body so nice?
There's flour in the bread, flour in the bread.
Energy's stored in each and every slice.
There's wonderful flour in the bread.

CHORUS:
There is flour, flour, healthy, wholesome flour in the bread, in the bread.
There is flour, flour, nutritious full-grain flour in that good old whole-wheat bread.

Original Words: Lewis E. Jones, 1899

## 'Tis So Sweet to Eat That Chocolate
(Tune: 'Tis So Sweet To Trust In Jesus)

'Tis so sweet to eat that chocolate. Yes it is a great delight
Just to sit and stuff it down, to savor each and every bite.

'Tis so sweet to eat that chocolate in ice cream, puddings, cakes and pies.
Candy bars and fudge I cherish. Even eat it on my fries!

'Tis so sweet to eat that chocolate, morning, noontime or at night.
No matter what the occasion how it makes my spirit bright.

Chocolate in my favorite snack. Chocolate in the milk I drink.
If I couldn't have my chocolate in depression I would sink.

CHORUS:
Chocolate, chocolate, how I love it. I've devoured it o'er and o'er.
Chocolate, chocolate, precious chocolate. I can't wait to eat some more.

Original Words: Louisa M. R. Stead, 1882

# When the Rolls Are Served With Butter
(Tune: When the Roll Is Called Up Yonder)

When the dinner bell at last shall sound and so our work shall cease,
And those wonderful aromas fill the air,
When the hungry folks shall gather to the table for to feast,
And the rolls are served with butter I'll be there.

On that big and well-spread table filled with vegetables and fruit,
And cranberry sauce and bread and cheese to spare,
When the turkey's filled with stuffing and the dumpling's in the soup,
And the rolls are served with butter I'll be there.

Let us savor every mouthful and enjoy each tasty bite.
Every morsel is delicious I declare.
When with thanks we all shall gather for to feast on such delight,
And the rolls are served with butter I'll be there.

CHORUS:
When the rolls are served with butter,
"How delicious" tongues will utter.
Everyone will want another.
When the rolls are served with butter I'll be there.

Original Words: James M. Black, 1893

# Wonderful Taste of Peanuts
(Tune: Wonderful Grace of Jesus)

Wonderful taste of peanuts. Surely it is a sin.
How shall my tongue describe it? Where shall its praise begin?
Taking away my hunger, oh so deliciously.
For the wonderful taste of peanuts pleases me.

Wonderful taste of peanuts whene'er my taste buds cry,
Morning or noon or evening my craving will satisfy.
Shelled, honey roasted, Spanish, salted, I'm on a spree.
For the wonderful taste of peanuts pleases me.

Wonderful taste of peanuts. Addicted I can't deny.
Oh, for another fix. Oh yes, for a fresh supply.
Maybe you think I'm crazy. I cannot disagree,
But the wonderful taste of peanuts pleases me.

CHORUS:
Wonderful the matchless taste of peanuts, better far than walnuts or cashews.
Wonderful taste so delicious for you, for me and you.
[Tasty on a mountain, or beside a fountain,
We love to eat them down, both me and you.]
More scrumptious than hazelnuts or filberts.
Sweeter far than almonds or pecans.
Oh, sing of the delicious taste of peanuts. Eat them down!

Original Words: Haldor Lillines, 1918

## Pot Pies for Christ
(Tune: Not I, But Christ)

Pot pies for Christ, my honored, loved, exalted.
Pot pies for Christ, oh, let the song be heard.
Pot pies for Christ, if salted or unsalted.
Pot pies for Christ, our every thought and word.

Pot pies for Christ, in lowly, silent labor.
Pot pies for Christ, in humble, earnest toil.
Pot pies for Christ. Oh, join in every neighbor.
Pot pies for Christ, bake them before they spoil.

Pot pies for Christ, his every need supplying.
Pot pies for Christ, his strength and health to be.
Pot pies for Christ, let's bake them without sighing.
Pot pies for Christ, to eat eternally.

Pot pies for Christ, if chicken, beef or turkey.
Pot pies for Christ, to please our lord so fine.
Pot pies for Christ, much better than beef jerky.
Pot pies for Christ, better than eating swine.

CHORUS:
Oh, to be saved from myself, dear lord.
Oh, to make pies for thee.
Oh, that it might be no more cakes.
Pot pies I bake for thee.

Original Words: Albert B. Simpson, Ada A. Whiddington

## Dancing, Dancing
(Tune: Praise Him! Praise Him!)

Dancing, dancing, oh how I love to go dancing.
It fills me, thrills me, makes my spirit feel light.
Contras, polkas, international folk,
English country is to my heart a delight.
Ballroom, squares, circles and lines and sets.
And with rock and roll you cannot go wrong.

Dancing, dancing, oh how I love to go dancing.
When I move with music I'm happy and free.
With a partner or just as a part of the group,
Or by myself I'm happy and full of glee.
Pivoting, leaping, twirling and walking and bouncing.
Promenading, marching and joining in song.

CHORUS:
Dancing, dancing, oh how I love to go dancing.
Dancing, dancing, come won't you join along.

Original Words: Fanny Crosby, 1869

## Since I Have Eaten Ice Cream
(Tune: Since I Have Been Redeemed)

I have a song I love to sing since I have eaten ice cream,
Of a creamy, sweet, refreshing thing since I have eaten ice cream.

I have a joy I can't express since I have eaten ice cream,
When to an ice cream parlor I progress since I have eaten ice cream.

I have a home where I love to go since I have eaten ice cream.
To savor chocolate marshmallow since I have eaten ice cream.

I have a witness bright and clear since I have eaten ice cream.
That coffee cones are so very dear since I have eaten ice cream.

I have a flavor that satisfies since I have eaten ice cream.
A scoop of mocha chip always takes the prize since I have eaten ice cream.

CHORUS:
Since I have eaten ice cream,
Since I have eaten ice cream I will eat it every day.
Since I have eaten ice cream I'll enjoy a bowl of it today.

Original Words: E. O. Excell

## Music, Music, Music
(Tune: He Keeps Me Singing)

There's within my heart a melody. How I love to sing it so.
It keeps my spirit feeling light and free in all of life's ebb and flow.

All my life was wrecked, my spirit cried, and my heart was filled with pain,
But the music reached me deep inside, stirred the slumbering chords again.

I thrill to hear melodies arrive. When I hear the harmony ring
The rhythm really makes me feel alive. That is why I shout and sing.

Though sometimes I tread through waters deep, trials fall across my way,
Though sometimes the path seems rough and steep, music always smooths the way.

Soon the music sets my feet to move. My arms and hips are soon in gear.
I break into dance. My mood improves. All my troubles disappear.

CHORUS:
Music, music, music, sweetest sound I know.
Fills my soul with laughter. Keeps me singing as I go.

Original Words: Luther B. Bridgers, 1910

## Saving and Serving

Saving and serving our watchword shall sound.
Saving the ball to keep it in bounds.
Serving it straight and true with a nice, hard swat.
Serving the ball and saving the shot.

Serving the ball so straight and so true.
Once in a while we try an angle new.
Trying to send it in there burning hot,
Without having it hit the net and go "Splot!"

Saving the ball -- come and now teach
How to save that ball when it's hard to reach.
Keeping it in play so we can all have fun
No matter who loses or who has won.

CHORUS:
Serving the ball and saving the shot.
Wiping off the sweat and cleaning out the snot.
Keep us blessed master, set for the onslaught.
Serving the ball and saving the shot.

Original Words: Albert Benjamin Simpson, 1903

## Paddling My Kayak on the Great Blue Sea
(Tune: Leaning on the Everlasting Arms)

What experience, what a joy so fine,
Paddling my kayak on the great blue sea.
What exuberance, what a peace is mine,
Paddling my kayak on the great blue sea.

Oh, how sweet to adventure in this way,
Paddling my kayak on the great blue sea.
Oh, how fun the sea grows from day to day,
Paddling my kayak on the great blue sea.

What have I to dread? What have I to fear,
Paddling my kayak on the great blue sea.
I have peace of heart with my paddle near,
Paddling my kayak on the great blue sea.

CHORUS:
Paddling, paddling, happy, content and, oh, so free.
Paddling, paddling, paddling my kayak on the great blue sea.

Original Words: E. A. Hoffman, 1887

## Jesus Played Baseball
(Tune: Jesus Paid It All)

I heard the savior say, "I like to play baseball.
Let me join your team today, and your games, you'll win them all."

The team was desperate. They let him play that day.
Then a big home run he hit in the third inning they played.

The ball sailed out of the field. The crowd, they just went wild.
You should've heard just how they squealed when Jesus at them smiled.

CHORUS:
Jesus played baseball, played shortstop and third.
Hit a big home run one day, and what a buzz he stirred.

Original Words: Elvina M. Hall, 1865

> *You believe in a book that has talking animals, wizards, witches, demons, sticks turning into snakes, burning bushes, food falling from the sky, people walking on water and all sorts of magical, absurd and primitive stories, and you say that we are the ones that need help?*      -- Mark Twain

## What a Joy There Is in Hiking
(Tune: What a Friend We Have in Jesus)

What a joy there is in hiking, getting up at five o'clock.
Hit that trail before your system realizes that it is in shock.
What the hell is the sun doing up at this hour of the morning anyway?
You can't think about that now, though, for you must be on your way.

What a joy there is in hiking, finding wildlife everywhere.
Wasps, mosquitoes, flies and minges all the way your path will share.
They will keep you so amused that you won't get bored along the way.
Every moment of your journey you'll have someone with whom to play.

What a joy there is in hiking, starting in the cool of morn
When a mere lightweight jacket with three sweaters must be worn.
Then the sun comes out to greet you, warm you with its rays so bright.
Draw the sweat out from your forehead, with its heat your spirit smite.

What a joy there is in hiking, getting healthy exercise
Stretching out those unused muscles in legs, ankles, knees and thighs.
Feel them ache and scream in protest up and over every rise
'Til you're totally exhausted, and you're almost paralyzed.

Original Words: Joseph Medlicott Scriven, 1855

## Step By Step

'Tis so sweet to climb a mountain, step by step and all the way,
Climbing ever upward, forward, 'til at the top my pack I lay.

I may tire as I travel, my legs feel like they have to stop,
But this challenge I must meet. Keep on stepping to the top.

Now I'm drawing closer, closer, to the top, my goal, my aim.
My pace now quickens, my pack seems lighter. I hurry 'til the top I claim.

When I reach the peak so high and all the world below me lay,
The thrill of victory I'll savor, and I'll sing this song so gay.

CHORUS:
Step by step, with lots of pep, this mountain I will climb.
All the way, no delay, to the top in record time.

Original Words: Albert B. Simpson

## Is Thy Heart Right in Thy Bod
(Tune: Is Thy Heart Right With God)

Does your aorta and ventricle cross? Is thy heart right in thy bod?
Do you now suffer from blood pressure loss? Is thy heart right in thy bod?

Do you eat many foods with lots of fat? Is thy heart right in thy bod?
Or healthy foods that make it go pitter pat? Is thy heart right in thy bod?

Do you get lots of good exercise? Is thy heart right in thy bod?
Keeping blood flowing so you'll have bright eyes? Is thy heart right in thy bod?

CHORUS:
Is thy heart right in thy bod? Beating without rhythm odd,
Solid, not holey, beating nice and slowly, nice and right tight in thy bod?

Original Words: Elisha A. Hoffman, 1899

## I Need Pee Every Hour
(Tune: I Need Thee Every Hour)

I need pee every hour. Oh, my good gracious lord!
My bladder is so weak that not much can be stored.

I need pee every hour. I can't sleep thru the night.
I must get up to pee. Oh, what an awful plight!

I need pee every hour. Damn excretory gland.
I always make sure the bathroom is at hand.

I need pee every hour. No matter what I do,
I'm always making trips both to and from the loo.

CHORUS:
I need pee. Oh, I need pee. Every hour I need pee.
Oh, bless me now my savior. I need to pee.

<sub>Original Words: Annie S. Hawks (1872); Robert Lowry (1872)</sub>

# Sneeze! Sneeze! Sneeze!
### (Tune: Saved, Saved, Saved)

Sneeze! Sneeze! Sneeze! I cannot help but sneeze.
All this pollen makes me start to wheeze.
Once the allergy season comes around
Listen close and you will hear this sound.

Sneeze! Sneeze! Sneeze! Oh, morning, noon and night.
Yes, it surely is an awful plight.
Blowing here and blowing over there.
One may strike at anytime. Beware!

Sneeze! Sneeze! Sneeze! What can a person do?
Oh, it has me feeling awful blue.
No matter what I do or where I go
One may strike. Watch out! Here comes a blow.

CHORUS:
Sneeze, I sneeze, when pollen fills the air.
Sneeze, I sneeze. My allergy does flair.
I tried to hold it in before, but out it came with a great big roar!
I keep on sneezing o'er and o'er. I sneeze, sneeze, sneeze!

<sub>Original Words: Oswald J. Smith, E. O. Excell</sub>

# Solar Power
### (Tune: Old Time Power)

We are gathered for thy blessing. Come now help us out, oh god,
The importance of green power stressing. Help create awareness broad.

We will glory in the power that we get from the sun's rays,
Many kilowatts per hour especially on sunny days.

As we come in prayer before thee help us and our souls inspire
To make lots of green energy from that yellow ball of fire.

CHORUS:
Spirit, now melt and move us the sun's worth to prove.
Help us get in the groove with solar power.

<sub>Original Words: Paul Rader, 1917</sub>

## Yield Not Perspiration
(Tune: Yield Not to Temptation)

Yield not perspiration, for yielding will smell.
Sweaty and pungent odors your friends will dispel.
Confidently go onward. All odors subdue.
Always wear antiperspirant; it will carry you through.

Shun perfumy odors. Strong fragrance disdain.
Use fresh, unscented brands or this will be in vain.
Be thoughtful, considerate of those around you.
Always wear antiperspirant; it will carry you through.

To him that o'ercometh, many friends will abound.
For she who remembers success will be found.
If you want lots of friends, success and influence too,
Always wear antiperspirant; it will carry you through.

CHORUS:
Antiperspirant will help you stay as fresh as the morning dew,
So you won't smell like the town zoo. It will carry you through.

Original Words: Horatio R. Palmer, 1868

## My Deodorant Holds
(Tune: My Anchor Holds)

Though the angry surges roll on my tempest driven soul,
I am peaceful for I know, wildly though the winds may blow,
I've a deodorant safe and "SURE" that will all the day endure.

Mighty tides about me sweep, perils lurk within the deep.
Angry clouds o'ershade the sky, and the tempest rises high.
Still I stand the tempest's shock. My deodorant still does block.

I can tell it's holding fast as I meet each sudden blast,
And the barrier, though unseen, keeps me ever smelling clean.
Thru the storm I safely ride, 'til the turning of the tide.

Troubles almost 'whelm the soul. Griefs like billows o'er me roll.
I do almost go astray. Storms obscure the light of day.
And yet still I can be bold. I've a deodorant that shall hold.

CHORUS:
And it holds my deodorant holds. Blow your wildest then, oh gale,
On my bark so small and frail. It is strong; it shall not fail.
For my deodorant holds, my deodorant holds.

Original Words: W. C. Martin

## We're Working Together
### (Tune: We're Marching to Zion)

Come we that love the earth and let our care be shown.
Let's join together hand in hand, to save our water, air and land
From those who pollute, despoil for profit of their own.

Let those refuse to sing whose profit is their god,
But children of the earth who care to preserve the earth so fair,
Will speak their concerns abroad, will speak their concerns abroad.

The earth we live on yields a wondrous beauty so fair,
With everything we need to thrive, and for all creatures to survive,
Oh, if we treat it with care, oh if we treat it with care.

Then let our songs abound and our resolve be seen
Our resources to not destroy, so that our children may enjoy
A world that's fair and clean, a world that's fair and clean.

CHORUS:
We're working together this fragile planet to save.
We'll work together to save this earth, the only home we have.

Original Words: Isaac Watts

## The Conflicts of the Ages
### (Tune: The Conflict of the Ages)

Lo the conflicts of the ages are still with us today.
The armies are assembled all in battle array.
Are you cheering for your own side for a victory to score,
Or have you come now to your senses and seen the horror of war?

Catch the vision of a new world without any war,
Where are killing and hatred tolerated no more.
See all children of the earth joined in their hearts and their hands.
To live in peace and love together with war forever banned.

See the nations now awakening with the firmest resolve
To come talk and work together all their problems to solve,
And to grant that all earth's peoples live in justice and peace
'Til the day, oh let it come, when all thoughts of war will cease.

CHORUS:
Have your eyes caught the vision? Are your hearts all affright?
Because war and destruction won't decide who is right.
For the conflicts of the ages, no matter who the battle wages,
Only cause us further hatred, sorrow, malice and spite.

Original Words: Lelia Neylor Morris

# Battle Hymn of the Republic

Mine eyes have seen the gory, bloody scenes of senseless war.
We are trampling on the people, decimating rich and poor.
We have loosed our fateful lightning to create great scenes of gore.
The lies are marching on.

I have seen the helpless people in their squalid refuge camps.
They do worry for their lives in the evening dews and damps
While I read of how our leaders claim to be their freedom's champs.
The lies are marching on.

I have read of how our leaders send our troops their oil to steal.
"Oh, if you resist our forces then great death to you we'll deal.
Let our hero, Son of Riches, crush your weak ones with his heel".
The lies are marching on.

We have sounded forth our threat'nings that we never will retreat.
We ignore all history while its ills we do repeat.
Oh, be swift our souls to answer to the words of great deceit.
The lies are marching on.

While in beauty we do live our war is waged across the sea.
We glory in our power. With their slaughter we agree.
We ignore their suff'ring, create world disharmony.
The lies are marching on.

We claim that they have weapons-of-mass-destruction in their midst.
We fix facts around the policy that just do not exist.
When that won't work we claim that they have ties to terrorists.
The lies are marching on.

We ignore the laws of nations -- cause our image to decay.
We spend our finite resources to get what we want today,
While we leave the massive debt for our grandchildren to repay.
The lies are marching on.

We claim that we won't conquer, only bring democracy.
Then we build our lasting presence – the world's biggest embassy.
While they die from bombs and bullets we save the oil ministry.
The lies are marching on.

To carry out our bidding we do send mercenaries.
They terrorize the people and create atrocities.
When they kill the innocents there's no accountability.
The lies are marching on.

Our poor and hungry suffer as we pay for all this grief.
Our schools and children languish. Our sick get no relief,
While the military contractors get rich beyond belief.
The lies are marching on.

How long will we continue list'ning to their flagrant lies?
How long before we realize their intentions they disguise?
When will we see it's truth and rule of law that they despise?
The lies are marching on.

Let's stop this senseless killing, end this travesty before
By every land and people the great U.S. is abhorred.
Let's stand up for integrity, demand that nevermore
Their lies go marching on.

CHORUS:
Gory, gory in Fallujah. Don't let the pow'rs that be delude ya.
Some day the violence will include ya. The lies are marching on.

Original Words: Julia Ward Howe, 1862

## Stand Up for Peace
(Tune: Stand Up for Jesus)

Stand up, stand up for peace. This is our sincere aim.
Lift up our banners high; the message we'll proclaim.
From vict'ry unto vict'ry together we'll proceed
'Til every war is ended and peace shall reign indeed.

Stand up, stand up for justice. All you from south to north
Lift up our voices high; the message will go forth.
From vict'ry unto vict'ry together we'll endure
'Til injustice has been vanquished and everyone's secure.

Stand up stand up for the earth, no matter what's occurred.
Lift up our spirits high; the message will be heard.
From vict'ry unto vict'ry together we will toil
'Til earth at last is safe for all who will walk its soil.

Original Words: George Duffield 1858

## Soldiers of Peace, Arise!
(Tune: Soldiers of Christ, Arise!)

Soldiers of peace, arise and put your swords away,
Strong in the strength which is supplied when love we will obey.
Strong in your firm resolve to live in harmony
That every woman, man and child from violence may be free.

Stand then in this great might that selfless love instills,
And take to arm you what is right communication skills,
That when conflicts arise and tempers start to soar,
You can resolve them peacefully without going to war.

Stand up for human rights for everyone alive,
Determined that no human being's rights they will deprive.
Oh, life and liberty, security enshrined,
Protected for all without distinction of any kind.

Original Words: Charles Wesley, 1749

# Amazing Grace

Amazing Grace, how sweet that girl that wrecked a wretch like me.
She caused my heart's desires to whirl, then from me she did flee.

'Twas Grace that caused my heart to cheer, and then again to cry.
How precious did that Grace appear when she my way passed by.

Oh, Grace once promised to be true. Her words my faith assured,
But then I found out that into her trap I had been lured.

She said I was the only one, and I her words believed
'Til I found out the tale she'd spun and knew I'd been deceived.

She used me, left me high and dry. Her heart is like a stone.
Yet still I cannot help but try to win her for my own.

Oh, many plans and plots and snares I have already tried.
She's eluded them with flair and will until I've died.

When I have tried for many years to win that girl so fair
I will drown in all my tears, and she won't even care.

Original Words: John Newton, 1779


# I Love to Tell a Story
### (Tune: I Love to Tell the Story)

I love to tell a story of things you wouldn't believe,
Of which a sane sound person couldn't possibly conceive.
I love to tell a story, whether or not it's true.
It satisfies my ego as nothing else can do.

I love to tell a story. More wonderful it seems
Than all our golden fancies, than all your golden dreams.
I love to tell a story. It does so much for me,
And that is just the reason I tell it now to thee

I love to tell a story. 'Tis pleasant to repeat.
Each time I do I tell of a more incredible feat.
I love to tell a story, for some have never heard
Of events so unbelievable as those I swear occurred.

CHORUS:
I love to tell a story. It is my greatest glory
To tell a big, tall story and everyone believe it's true.

Original Words: Kate Hankey (1866); William G. Fischer (1869) (refrain)

# Fire Hound
(Tune: Higher Ground)

I'm working in a fireman's way. New fires I'm quenching every day,
Still spraying on each fire I've found, but I wish I had a fire hound.

My heart has no desire to spray where little fires cause no dismay.
Oh, let me spray when flames abound, but give to me a fire hound.

I want to tame the fire's height and fight against those flames so bright.
I'll keep on fighting 'til I've found a brave trustworthy fire hound.

CHORUS:
A nice big dog with me to stand as I do fight each fire so grand.
No better help ever I've found. Oh, give to me a fire hound.

Original Words: Johnson Oatman, Jr.

# There Shall Be Plowers Undressing
(Tune: There Shall Be Showers of Blessing)

There shall be plowers undressing. This is the promise of love.
No longer their plows they're pressing. No longer their plows they shove.

There shall be plowers undressing. Precious reviving again.
See how just now they're expressing how proud they are to be men.

There shall be plowers undressing. Send them upon us, oh lord.
Give us a show interesting, so that we won't be so bored.

There shall be plowers undressing, if they will our calls obey.
No longer urges repressing, let them their bodies display.

CHORUS:
Plowers undressing. Plowers undressing we need.
Others are taking their clothes off, but for the plowers we plead.

Original Words: D. W. Whittle, 1883

# Part 2

## Songs for Most Everyone

Probably not too objectionable. Can share with your Christian friends if they are not too persnickety.

# Oh, Job, He Is My Man
### (Tune: Launch Out)

*And the LORD said unto Satan, Hast thou considered my servant Job, that there is none like him in the earth, a perfect and an upright man, one that feareth God, and escheweth evil? - Job 1:8*

Oh, Job was an upright and virtuous man
Who made the lord feel, oh so proud.
God wagered the devil could not get him to sin
So to old Satan he vowed,

So they took away everything Job had
And left him helpless and poor,
But Job didn't sin or curse god bad
So god said to Satan once more,

One day Job's children at home did abide.
To kill them Satan made a threat.
"Go ahead and kill them if you wish," god replied,
"It's just part of our nice little bet."

When that didn't work Satan came back to say,
"Just strike him with sores head to toe,"
"Why not?" god said, "Just one more play
In our fun little wager, you know."

Well, god gave back everything Job had
Once he had had all his fun.
He even replaced his kids with some more,
So no harm in the end had been done.

CHORUS:
"Oh, Job, he is my man. Go ahead and hit him cruel.
Take all that he has. Kill his kids. Strike him sore.
Do your best you losing fool!"

Original Words: A. B. Simpson, 1891

# Send the Fire
### (Tune: Send Refreshing)

*And Elijah answered and said to the captain of fifty, If I be a man of God, then let fire come down from heaven, and consume thee and thy fifty. And there came down fire from heaven, and consumed him and his fifty. -- 2 Kings 1:10*

Fifty men came to bring Elijah to the king of Israel.
Elijah called down fire from heaven. Cooked them suckers up right swell.

Fifty more came to Elijah, his person again to invite.
Again he called down fire from heaven to burn them all with great delight.

Heavenly father, we your children know how you are so cruel.
Send your fire on those who hate us. Send them right straight down to hell!

CHORUS:
Send the fire! Send the fire, from thy presence, vicious lord!
Send the fire! Send the fire! Light things up -- we're getting bored!

Original Words: Daniel Webster Whittle

# Harden Pharaoh's Heart
(Tune: Let My People Go / Go Down Moses)

When Israel was in Egypt's land. Harden Pharaoh's heart!
Oh, god had death and suffering planned. Harden Pharaoh's heart!

God turned the Nile right into blood. Harden Pharaoh's heart!
Then hardened his heart. He said "Oh crud!" Harden Pharaoh's heart!

Oh, god sent frogs on everyone. Harden Pharaoh's heart!
Then hardened his heart when he was done. Harden Pharaoh's heart!

Oh, swarms of lice then god sent next. Harden Pharaoh's heart!
Then hardened his heart like he was hexed. Harden Pharaoh's heart!

Then god sent flies to plague them all. Harden Pharaoh's heart!
So much fun! God was having a ball. Harden Pharaoh's heart!

Then all the livestock god struck dead. Harden Pharaoh's heart!
Then hardened his heart to continue the dread. Harden Pharaoh's heart!

Their bodies god then struck with sores. Harden Pharaoh's heart!
Then hardened his heart so he could do more. Harden Pharaoh's heart!

Then god sent hail big enough to kill. Harden Pharaoh's heart!
Then hardened his heart so he could do his will. Harden Pharaoh's heart!

Then locust came to devour their crops. Harden Pharaoh's heart!
But he hardened his heart. He wasn't going to stop. Harden Pharaoh's heart!

Then god sent darkness deep and cold. Harden Pharaoh's heart!
And hardened his heart his deadly plan to unfold. Harden Pharaoh's heart!

Then every first-born child god killed. Harden Pharaoh's heart!
When he saw them dead he was, oh, so thrilled. Harden Pharaoh's heart!

So come to our god of love, so swell. Harden Pharaoh's heart!
So he can harden your heart and send you to hell. Harden Pharaoh's heart!

CHORUS:
Go down, Moses! Go talk to old Pharaoh.
I'll harden his heart, so he won't let my people go.

Original Words: Traditional spiritual

## Grace That Killed Others for David's Sin
(Tune: Grace Greater Than Our Sin)

*Howbeit, because by this deed thou hast given great occasion to the enemies of the LORD to blaspheme, the child also that is born unto thee shall surely die. -- 2 Samuel 12:14*
*So the LORD sent a pestilence upon Israel from the morning even to the time appointed: and there died of the people from Dan even to Beersheba seventy thousand men. - 2 Samuel 24:15*

David was the king of Israel,
A man who followed each of god's goals,
Except when he didn't, and then came hell,
Though not to David but to innocent souls.

David once slept with another's wife.
Pregnant she got. He said all so snide,
"No problem. I'll just take her man's life
and take Bathsheba as my own bride."

God then was mad at what he did see.
Punishment he said he would enact.
Did he hurt David, give him leprosy?
No, he killed the child for David's act.

David once numbered the Israelites.
For some reason god's anger did stoke.
He sent his wrath in a manner so right.
Killed seventy thousand guiltless folk.

CHORUS:
Grace, grace, god's grace. Grace is the way that these tales we'll spin.
Grace, grace, god's grace. Grace that killed others for David's sin.

Original Words: Julia H. Johnston, 1911

## Send the Fire!
(Tune: Send the Light!)

*Then the LORD rained upon Sodom and upon Gomorrah brimstone and fire from the LORD out of heaven. -- Genesis 19:24*

Oh, Sodom and Gomorrah were two cities past. Send the fire! Send the fire!
They were so evil they just burned god's ass. Send the fire! Send the fire!

Oh, Sodom was full of evil Sodomites. Send the fire! Send the fire!
The kind of people god just loves to smite. Send the fire! Send the fire!

The men of Sodom were a sorry mess. Send the fire! Send the fire!
They wanted to have some sex with Lot's guests. Send the fire! Send the fire!

But Lot was a man who had a righteous soul. Send the fire! Send the fire!
He offered his daughters for the Sodomites' goal. Send the fire! Send the fire!

CHORUS:
Send the fire down on those folks so wild. Let it burn them everyone,
Every man and woman, dog and child. Cook them 'til they are well done.

Original Words: Charles H. Gabriel, 1890

# The Fire Is Burning

I've now seen Gomorrah's fiery light.
A nice barbeque is my heart's desire.
I have glimpsed of Sodom glowing bright.
Oh, let's go roast hotdogs in the fire.

I will sit with Jesus, bless his name.
Together we will watch the flames grow higher.
We just love to watch a nice, big flame
And roast up hotdogs in the fire.

God did send his fire upon those towns.
He burned them up just like a pile of tires.
Gave what serves them right, those foolish clowns,
So we could roast hotdogs in the fire.

CHORUS:
Oh, the fire is burning. Yes, 'tis brightly burning,
What a nice big bonfire out of doors.
Oh, the fire is burning. Yes, 'tis brightly burning.
Toast up marshmallows and make some s'mores.

Original Words: Johnson Oatman

# 'Tis Burning in Their Streets
(Tune: 'Tis Burning in My Soul)

God sent his mighty fire to Sodom's sinful farts.
Lit them up like a pyre, his great grace to impart.
And since his fire came to cook them up like meat
The love-enkindled flame is burning in their streets.

Almighty god above, he can do anything.
He could have shown his love, a peaceful message bring.
Instead, in his great ire he roasted them complete.
Oh, god's beloved fire is burning in their streets.

The gracious god above is loving, so they say,
But he displays his love in a very strange way.
If you kindle his ire with wrath you he will treat.
And you will find his fire is burning in your streets.

CHORUS:
'Tis burning in their streets. 'Tis burning in their streets.
The fire of heavenly love is burning in their streets.
Oh, Sodom's children burn. Gomorrah's kids in turn.
The fire of heavenly love is burning in their streets.

Original Words: Delia T. White

## Tell Me the Story of Jacob
(Tune: Tell Me the Story of Jesus)

*And Esau said to Jacob, Feed me, I pray thee, with that same red pottage; for I am faint: ... And Jacob said, Sell me this day thy birthright. Genesis 25:30-31*

Tell me the story of Jacob. Write on my heart every word.
Tell me the story outrageous, vilest that ever was heard,
How he stole his brother's birthright, blackmailed him when he was weak,
Took advantage when he was starving, his own greedy gain to seek.

Tell how he stole Esau's blessing, lying to his blind old dad.
When I hear how he took advantage it makes me feel, oh, so glad.
Makes me admire the lord who made the great nation of god
From a sly shyster and swindler who loved to cheat and defraud.

I know how to treat my brothers and my sisters in the lord.
I have example to follow right out of god's precious word.
I'll be like god's servant Jacob, learn how to lie and defraud,
Blackmail them when chance arises, thus gaining favor from our god.

CHORUS:
Tell me the story of Jacob, Israel, the chosen of god,
So I'll know how to treat my brothers, how to swindle and defraud.

Original Words: Fanny Crosby, 1880

## Just Look at Him Sway Pretty
(Tune: His Way With Thee)

Would you look at Jesus and see how he dances good?
Moves with so much flair, swings those hips the way he should?
Just admire the way he moves with grace, if you would.
Just look at him sway pretty.

Would you learn to dance with style at each and every ball?
Learn to prance and strut, and never have to fall?
Just watch now our Jesus dance, impressing one and all.
Just look at him sway pretty.

Would you look at Jesus as with rhythm he does move?
Moves those nimble hips, just gets into the groove?
Walks with poise, and turns with grace? He glides ever so smooth.
Just look at him sway pretty.

CHORUS:
His moves can show you how it ought to be.
His flair will turn you so green with envy.
His style will make you gasp, and you will be
Impressed to just look at him sway pretty.

Original Words: Cyrus S. Nusbaum, 1898

## Underwear for Jesus
(Tune: Anywhere With Jesus)

Underwear for Jesus I can safely sew.
Underwear he can safely wear below.
Underwear of quality that will not fade.
Underwear for Jesus. I am not afraid.

Underwear for Jesus on the land or sea,
So even when half-dressed he will pretty be.
Underwear to wear for him to go or stay.
Underwear for Jesus so he's dressed the right way.

Underwear for Jesus when he goes to sleep,
Or when 'round the neighborhood he goes to creep.
Underwear wherever he goes out to roam
Or when he just hangs out at his home, sweet home.

CHORUS:
Underwear. Underwear. Every stitch I know.
Underwear for Jesus I can safely sew.

Original Words: Jessie Brown Pounds, 1887; Helen C. A. Dixon, 1910

## I've Won the Disgrace of Jesus
(Tune: Wonderful Grace of Jesus)

I've won the disgrace of Jesus by doing lots of sin.
How shall my tongue describe it? Where shall its praise begin?
Now I'm no longer burdened. My sinful spirit's free.
For I've won the disgrace of Jesus. Good gracious me!

I've won the disgrace of Jesus. Forgive me if I boast
Of all the stunts I've pulled off, sinned to the uttermost.
From him I'm torn asunder, giving me liberty.
For I've won the disgrace of Jesus. Good gracious me!

I've won the disgrace of Jesus. My soul is so defiled,
But I'm so happy that way, playing like a little child.
Now Jesus has disowned me for all eternity.
For I've won the disgrace of Jesus. Good gracious me!

CHORUS:
I've won the much esteemed disgrace of Jesus.
It makes me want to laugh and roll with glee.
Wonderful is his disgrace upon me, oh even me.
[Greater than a mountain, dancing like a fountain,
I love to make him disgraced with me.]
Broad is sure the scope of my transgressions.
Sin just doesn't bring me any shame.
I'm having so much fun and so I'll keep on raising Cain!

Original Words: Haldor Lillines, 1918

## Lo, He Drums With Clowns Unending
(Tune: Lo, He Comes With Clouds Descending)

Lo, he drums with clowns unending, beating on those drums insane,
Thousand thousand clowns attending, listening to his rhythmic strain.
Alleluia! Alleluia! With his drums he'll sure raise Cain.

Every eye shall now behold him drumming with such majesty,
As the clowns just hoot and scold him, and they laugh aloud with glee.
Deeply wailing, deeply wailing on those drums so skillfully.

Now that drummer long expected see in clownish pomp appear.
With his rhythm we're infected, and those clowns just dance so queer.
Alleluia! Alleluia! How it fills us with such cheer.

Original Words: Charles Wesley, 1758

## Jesus Loves Even Fleas
(Tune: Jesus Loves Even Me)

I am so glad that our father in heav'n
Tells of his love in the book he has giv'n.
Wonderful things in the Bible I see.
This is the queerest that Jesus loves fleas.

Though I forget him and wander away
He'll send some fleas to wherever I stray.
Why does he do it? I swear he's a sleaze
When I remember that Jesus loves fleas.

Oh, if there's only one song I can sing
When in his beauty I see the great king,
This shall my song then waft over the breeze,
"Why in tarnation does Jesus love fleas?"

CHORUS:
I am so sad that Jesus loves fleas, Jesus loves fleas, Jesus loves fleas.
I am so sad that Jesus loves fleas, Jesus loves even fleas.

Original Words: Emily S. Oakey; P. P. Bliss, 1871

## Constantly He's Hiding
(Tune: Constantly Abiding)

There's a fellow who likes to play hide-and-go-seek,
But he is not much fun, because
No matter how hard you try to get a peek,
He's as real as the Wizard of Oz.

All the world seems to sing of a savior they know.
They claim that he treats them right swell.
But then when you do ask them that savior to show
He just seems to be hiding real well.

Maybe someday I'll meet this old fellow so queer
When he does come out from hiding.
Maybe we can sit down and chat over a beer,
And a little karaoke sing.

CHORUS:
Constantly he's hiding, Jesus so blind.
Constantly he's hiding, joker divine.
He always leaves me lonely. Never him you'll find.
Whenever you need him he'll leave you behind.

Original Words: Anne S. Murphy, 1908

# Jesus Shaves!
(Tune: Jesus Saves!)

We have heard the joyful sound: Jesus shaves! Jesus shaves!
Spread the tidings all around: Jesus shaves! Jesus shaves!
Bear the news to every land. Climb the mountains, cross the waves.
No more whickers on the man! Jesus shaves! Jesus shaves!

Waft it on the rolling tide: Jesus shaves! Jesus shaves!
Tell to shavers far and wide: Jesus shaves! Jesus shaves!
Sing, you islands of the sea. Echo back, you ocean caves.
Never more is he stubbly. Jesus shaves! Jesus shaves!

Give the winds a mighty voice: Jesus shaves! Jesus shaves!
Let the nations now rejoice: Jesus shaves! Jesus shaves!
Shaving cream to lubricate on skin convex or concave.
Every hair eliminate! Jesus shaves! Jesus shaves!

Original Words: Priscilla J. Owens

# Step by Step

'Tis so sweet to walk with Jesus, step by step and day by day,
'Til my knees are sore and tired, and I rub them with Bengay.

It's unsafe to walk with Jesus, bewitched by his magic charm,
Until he leads us off the cliff, where we fall to major harm.

Step by step I'll walk with Jesus, and I'll have a gay old time,
Because talking to myself is something I find sublime.

Jesus, would you please come closer. I can't see your blessed face.
For that matter, evidence that you exist I find no trace.

CHORUS:
Step by step, step by step, I would walk with Jesus,
All the day, all the way, off the cliff with Jesus.

Original Words: Albert B. Simpson

## Is My Name Written There?

Lord, I care not for riches, neither silver nor gold.
I want to get the furniture from my house that you stole.
On the back of that fine mahogany chair so fair,
Tell me, Jesus, you villain, is my name written there?

Lord, thy sins, they are many like the sands of the sea,
Even worse since you started on this thieving spree,
But since you broke in and my furniture stole
I now realize you're nothing but a troublesome troll.

Oh, that beautiful city with its mansions of light,
With its glorified beings, faces painted all white,
In the rooms of those mansions with their furniture fair,
Tell me, Jesus, you villain, you got it from where?

CHORUS:
Is my name written there on the back of that chair
That you stole from my house? Is my name written there?

Original Words: Mary A. Kidder

## 'Twas a Bad Day When Jesus Found Me
(Tune: 'Twas a Glad Day When Jesus Found Me)

I enjoyed my sin when Jesus found me,
Came to rescue me, what stupid crock so lame.
So I told him to go away, not hound me.
Didn't want to play his silly game.

Oh, the bells of churches now are ringing,
As to advertise their nonsense they do toll,
But my heart is filled with joyful singing.
I ignore their fool-hearted droll.

Oh, the joy when we shall turn, oh glory,
And their religion up their asses shove,
And we'll end their fool, ridiculous story
Of a savior's redeeming love.

CHORUS:
'Twas a bad day when Jesus found me,
When his mad people did surround me.
When my sins they tried to take away from me
And replace them with their hollow piety.
'Twas a bad day, a tale so sorry.
'Twas a bad day, I bitch and moan.
I will shout a glad hosanna in glory
When they finally leave me alone.

Original Words: Albert Simpson Reitz

## What If It Were Today?

Jesus is coming to earth again. What if it were today?
We will sure have a good party then. What if it were today?
Coming to eat some nice chicken fried. Coming to go down the water slide.
Coming with pretty shirt tie-dyed. What if it were today?

Satan's dominion will then be o'er. What if it were today?
Roast up his head and his tail to make s'mores. What if it were today?
Then shall the dead in Christ arise, wipe out the eye crust from their eyes,
Gather to eat chocolate-coated flies. What if it were today?

Faithful and true would he find us here. What if it were today?
Ready to hand him a nice cold beer. What if it were today?
Signs of his coming sure multiply. On Highway Thirty I did one spy.
Several along the freeway lie. What if it were today?

CHORUS:
Glory, glory! Joy to my heart 'twill bring.
Glory, glory! We'll have a grand old fling.
Glory, glory! Haste to prepare the way.
Glory, glory! Jesus will with us play!

Original Words: Mrs. C. H. Morris, 1912

> *God's only excuse is that he doesn't exist. - Stendahl*

## Christ Is Coming

*Verily I say unto you, There be some standing here, which shall not taste of death, till they see the Son of man coming in his kingdom. -- Matthew 16:28*

In the glow of early morning, in the solemn hush of night,
Down from heaven's open portals steals a messenger of light.
Jesus comes the Bible tells us. Just listen to its sweet tune.
We don't have much time to wait now. Christ is coming, coming soon.
Only twenty centuries or so. Christ is coming, coming soon.

Paul told us in his letters. James and Peter told us, too.
The apostles affirmed it strongly. Bible writers claimed 'twas true.
Some who heard him would not die, no, would not need to build a tomb.
Soon in Jesus would soar. Christ is coming, coming soon.
Just a few millennia more. Christ is coming, coming soon.

Jesus told us when he was with us. He for sure could not be wrong.
He'd return to get them someday. He'd come back. Would not be long.
Jesus was coming right quickly. Ere you knew before you he'd loom.
The day of his return it draws near. Christ is coming, coming soon.
Just two or three thousand years. Christ is coming, coming soon.

Original Words: W. Macomber

## He Played Hell With My Soul
(Tune: It Is Well With My Soul)

For years Jesus Christ attended my way.
At least that is what I was told.
But now I see clearly so now I can say,
"He played hell, he played hell with my soul."

The years that I spent seeking god and his way
Did take such a big heavy toll.
But I have survived and can tell you today,
"He played hell, he played hell with my soul."

Oh, so many times I have wished that I could
Have back all the years that he stole.
So have care, my friend. Let it be understood,
He'll play hell, he'll play hell with your soul.

CHORUS:
He played hell with my soul.  He played hell, he played hell with my soul.

Original Words: Horatio Gates Spafford, 1873

## I Cower in Prayer
(Tune: Sweet Hour of Prayer)

I cower in prayer. I cower in prayer, talking to god who just does not care.
Sits high and mighty on his big throne. For all my wishes throws me a bone.
In seasons of distress and grief he offers no bit of relief.
Just leaves me trapped in his big snare while I waste my time in useless prayer.

I cower in prayer. I cower in prayer, wishing that he would my burden share.
Instead, he threatens to make me burn forever in hell if to reason I turn.
It makes me ask why I should place my faith in a god who won't show his face,
Trusting in one who is not there and wasting my time in useless prayer.

I cower in prayer. I cower in prayer and wonder why he just is not there.
The great good god of faithfulness turns out to be nothing but foolishness.
Whenever I try to seek his face I find it's all a big disgrace.
But if you find some time to spare you can waste it in much useless prayer.

Original Words: W. W. Walford, 1845

## Nor Silver nor Gold

Nor silver nor gold do I have enough to mention.
No riches of earth to cheer up my poor soul.
The story of the cross was a crafty invention
To give to the church what from poor folks they stole.

Nor silver nor gold get much of my attention.
Too busy I am trying just to survive.
Meanwhile it seems to be the church's intention
All silver and gold from the poor to deprive.

Nor silver nor gold do I have in retention.
To feed Jesus' church just keeps me, oh, so poor.
My efforts to get rich it just puts the wrench in,
So should I give up and just believe in Thor?

CHORUS:
I could use a lot more silver. I would love a little gold.
But the church, the church of Jesus, it does too much of it hold.

Original Words: James M. Gray

# Fill My Cow
## (Tune: Fill Me Now)

Hover o'er my cow, oh, spirit. Soothe her trembling heart and brow.
Fill her with thy very best grain. Come, oh, come and fill my cow.

Thou canst fill her, gracious spirit. I am sure that you know how.
Then she will give lots of fresh milk. Come, oh, come and fill her now.

I am weakness, full of weakness. I need that old cow to plow.
Give her lots of healthy cow food. Come, oh, come and fill her now.

CHORUS:
Fill my cow. Fill my cow. Jesus, come and fill my cow.
Fill her with thy nice fine chow. Come, oh come and fill my cow.

Original Words: Edward H. Stokes, 1879

# Take My Wife and Let Me Be
## (Tune: Take My Life and Let It Be)

Take my wife and let me be. I will give her all to thee.
You can have her whines and moans, her constant bitching and ceaseless groans,
Constant bitching and ceaseless groans.

Take my wife and let me be. Don't need her nagging constantly.
Finally, I will have some peace when all her complaints do cease,
When all her complaints do cease.

Take my wife, the one I love. Give her to that god above.
Let her constant bitching keep him busy so I can sleep,
Keep him busy so I can sleep.

Original Words: Frances Ridley Havergal, 1874

## God's Unaware of You
(Tune: God Will Take Care of You)

Be not dismayed whate'er betide. God's unaware of you.
No need from his awful smitings to hide. God's unaware of you.

Through days of toil when heart doth fail god's unaware of you.
He won't know if you end up in jail. God's unaware of you.

Nothing you need he will provide. God's unaware of you.
When you look for him he'll always hide. God's unaware of you.

No matter what trouble be the test god's unaware of you.
Remember that god is just a pest. God's unaware of you.

CHORUS:
God's unaware of you through every day, o'er all the way.
God's unaware of you, because there is no god.

Original Words: Cevilla D. Martin, 1904

## Praise God from Whom All Smitings Flow
(Tune: Praise God from Whom All Blessings Flow)

Praise god from whom all smitings flow.
Praise him and hold your head down low.
Praise him or your soul he will roast.
Praise him or you will be a ghost.

Original Words: Thomas Ken, 1674

## He Breedeth Fleas, Oh, Wretched Thought
(Tune: He Leadeth Me, O Blessed Thought)

He breedeth fleas, oh wretched thought. Oh, now with fleas my cat is fraught.
Whate'er I do, where'er I be, please keep god's fleas away from me.

His nasty fleas get on my dog. Sometimes they even get on my hog.
I don't get it. I fail to see just why god needs to breed those fleas.

Sometimes 'mid scenes of deepest gloom I see god's fleas coming in my room
To my chagrin, against all my pleas. Oh, god just keeps on breeding fleas.

CHORUS:
He breedeth fleas. He breedeth fleas. By his own hand he breedeth fleas.
Far away from him I would be, for by his hand he breedeth fleas.

Original Words: Joseph H. Gilmore, 1862

## There's a Snideness in God's Mercy
(Tune: There's a Wideness in God's Mercy)

There's a snideness in god's mercy, as much snideness as can be.
There's a blindness in god's justice that just leads to travesty.

God's great mercy he doth show when he drowns everyone alive.
His great justice is so twisted, kills the innocent for others' crimes.

God's great mercy is so wondrous, sends most of us to hell fire.
His justice is so astounding, kills and smites to soothe his ire.

There's a snideness in god's mercy. It just shows he doesn't care.
There's a blindness in god's justice. I'm ashamed his name to bear.

Original Words: Frederick William Faber, 1862

> *No man ever believes that the Bible means what it says; he is always convinced that it says what he means.        -- George Bernard Shaw*

## Pokey Is His Name
(Tune: Glory to His Name)

Down by the side of Candasco Creek, where all the elves and the leprechauns meet,
Lives a nice dragon with pointed feet. Pokey is his name.

The other dragons were big and strong. They breathed out fire so hot and long,
But little Pokey couldn't join along, 'cause Pokey couldn't shoot flame.

He huffed and puffed and he flailed about, but nothing came from his dragon snout.
Then he sat down and began to pout. 'Twas a frightful shame.

One day when Pokey had had enough he went to visit that rascal Puff,
Who showed him how to really huff and puff and shoot a nice hot flame.

Now little Pokey is quite a fright, shooting his flame both left and right,
Scaring the Christians both day and night. What a nice, fun game!

If you believe in this dragon fraud perhaps you'll believe in the word of god.
Either tale is just as flawed and certainly as lame.

CHORUS:
Pokey is his name. Pokey is his name.
He's a nice dragon with pointed feet. Pokey is his name.

Original Words: E. A. Hoffman, 1878

# My Anchor Holds

Though the crazy stories roll o'er my tempest driven soul,
I am peaceful, for I know, wildly though hot wind they blow,
I've an anchor safe and sure that can evermore endure.

Crazy myths about me sweep, and the fables, in they creep.
Superstition rises high, and religion tells its lie.
Still I stand the tempest's shock, and religion's lies I block.

I can feel the anchor fast as I meet each sudden blast.
And with logic I dispel their claims of heaven and hell.
Thru the storm I safely ride and religion cast aside.

CHORUS:
And it holds, my anchor holds. Blow your wildest, then, oh gale.
Oh yes, science shall prevail. Rationality won't fail.
For my anchor holds, my anchor holds.

Original Words: W. C. Martin

# Now I'm Coming Home
(Tune: Lord, I'm Coming Home)

I've wandered far away with god. Now I'm coming home.
Religion's paths too long I've trod. Now I'm coming home.

I've wasted many precious years. Now I'm coming home.
I remember them with bitter tears. Now I'm coming home.

From superstition I now have fled. Now I'm coming home.
I got religion out of my head. Now I'm coming home.

I'm tired of praying and going to church. Now I'm coming home.
Only to find myself left in the lurch. Now I'm coming home.

CHORUS:
Coming home. Coming home. Nevermore to roam.
No more to be a religious clone. Now I'm coming home.

Original Words: William J. Kirkpatrick, 1892

# Living in Sunlight
(Tune: Heavenly Sunlight)

Walking in sunlight all of my journey
Over the mountains, through the deep vale.
Jesus has said, "Come, live in my darkness,"
But I don't want to get stuck in his swale.

Shadows around me, shadows above me,
Logic and reason will be my guide.
Keeping away from Jesus' sad darkness,
No longer in ignorance will I hide.

In the bright sunlight, ever rejoicing,
Keeping away that scoundrel above,
Singing hymn parodies gladly I'm walking,
Doing the sinful things that I love.

CHORUS:
Living in sunlight, wonderful sunlight, loving the freedom to think so fine.
Living in sunlight, wonderful sunlight, no longer listen to religious whine.

Original Words: Henry J. Zelley, 1899

# Once for All

Free from religion, oh, happy condition, even if you are now a Christian.
If its damn foolishness does you appall you can be free from it once for all.

You can be free. There's no condemnation. No need for some silly fool salvation,
No need on your knees down to fall. Get rid of religion once for all.

"Children of god," what label appalling. If such foolishness your soul is galling,
If you don't want to trust in tales tall come and be free from it once for all.

CHORUS:
Once for all, oh, friend now believe it. Once for all, oh, Christian receive it.
Give up religion. The burden will fall. Come and be free from it once for all.

Original Words: P. P. Bliss

# Piece, Perfect Piece
(Tune: Peace, Perfect Peace)

Piece, perfect piece in a world with lots of grease.
My slice of pizza is a perfect piece.

Peace, perfect peace in this world of sin.
Peacefully I sin with a great big grin.

Piece, perfect piece in this world depraved.
A perfect piece of ass is just what I crave.

Peace, perfect peace in this dark world of woe.
No more religion, then that peace can flow.

Peace, perfect peace, in the world today.
No more religion. It's the peaceful way.

Original Words: Edward Henry Bickersteth, 1875

## Yesterday They Weren't So Clever
(Tune: Yesterday, Today, Forever)

Oh, how queer the spurious message naïve faith may claim.
Yesterday they weren't so clever. Will we be the same?
Once they thought he saved the sinful, healed the sick and lame.
Will we stop believing myths, or will we still be lame?

Jesus was the friend of sinners -- so they used to say.
He'd make you feel warm and fuzzy if to him you'd pray.
Nowadays I'd like to think we'd come to realize
Believing in old superstitions intelligence defies.

Myth and legend did sustain us in the days of yore.
Jupiter and Zeus and Jesus, Mithra, Krishna and Thor,
All were such exciting fellows in susceptive minds --
Smiting, healing, thunder peeling, and such pretty shrines.

CHORUS:
Yesterday they weren't so clever, but they weren't to blame.
Nowadays will we do better, or will we still be lame?
Will we still be lame? Will we still be lame?
Nowadays will we do better, or will we still be lame?

Original Words: Albert Benjamin Simpson

## They're Jazzing Up Their Brooms
(Tune: A Missionary Cry)

A hundred thousand souls a day are sweeping all their dirt away
In houses filled with gloom.
But now they start to make things bright. They make their tools a pretty sight.
They're jazzing up their brooms. They're jazzing up their brooms.

Oh, holy cripe! The people move their pretty brooms so nice and smooth.
They're sweeping up their rooms.
Oh, every time they sweep again they mark their brooms with fancy pens.
They're jazzing up their brooms. They're jazzing up their brooms.

And, now they sweep up all the crap that religion on them does slap.
Oh, watch how each broom zooms.
They sweep away with stylish things all the crap religion brings.
They're jazzing up their brooms. They're jazzing up their brooms.

CHORUS:
They're jazzing, jazzing up so gay in thousands day by day.
They're jazzing up their brooms. They're jazzing up their brooms.

Original Words: Albert B. Simpson

## The Conflicts of the Pages
(Tune: The Conflict of the Ages)

Lo, the conflicts of the pages are upon us today.
Contradictions are assembling, oh, and what an array!
Are you numbered with the simple, one of god's well-duped few,
Who accept such mad conundrums? Do you buy that wild spew?

Oh, the books of the Kings do present what might seem clear,
But First and Second Chronicles something else rather queer.
Oh, when? Where? How many were there? You'd really like to know.
It depends on to which chapter in the Bible you go.

Oh yes, Matthew tells us one thing and then Mark something new.
Then Luke does his own song sing, and John talks thru his shoe.
Oh, wouldn't it be nice if one story they'd tell.
Then I could believe the right one and save my soul from hell.

CHORUS:
Do you read with clear vision? Does your heart feel right ill
To see those contradictions that the Bible do fill?
For the conflicts of the pages told by prophets and by sages
Are so obvious and so gaping they are nothing but swill.

Original Words: Lelia Neylor Morris

## Draw Me Naked
(Tune: Draw Me Nearer)

Oh, an artist friend once asked me to pose so she could my picture paint.
But when she asked me to take off my clothes I suddenly felt quite faint.

She told me it was not such a big deal. People do this every day.
But no matter how much she gave her spiel I just found it hard to stay.

She then told me not to be ashamed. She tried to allay my fears.
She assured me that I would be framed so my sexy view appears.

So I boldly ripped off all my clothes, and I stood up tall and proud.
And so now I have a picture that shows everything I was endowed.

When she finished with her art I paid her for it all,
And sent it to my mama, so smart, to hang on her front wall.

CHORUS:
Draw me naked, naked, oh my lord! I must take off everything.
Draw me naked, naked, naked, oh my lord! How can I do this thing?

Original Words: Fanny Crosby, 1875

# Let Us Break Heads Together, If You Please
(Tune: Let Us Break Bread Together on Our Knees)

Let us break heads together, if you please (if you please).
Let us break heads together, if you please (if you please).
When I knock you on your knees so that they are then well skun,
Oh lord, have mercy on me!

Let us break wind together in the breeze (in the breeze).
Let us break wind together in the breeze (in the breeze).
When I fart into the wind with my ass to the rising sun,
Oh lord, have mercy on me!

Let us shake heads together while we tease (while we tease).
Let us shake heads together while we tease (while we tease).
When I taunt and I tease to have such a lot of fun,
Oh lord, have mercy on me!

Let us take meds together while we wheeze (while we wheeze).
Let us take meds together while we wheeze (while we wheeze).
When I gasp and I wheeze and my nose with snot does run,
Oh lord, have mercy on me!

Let us bake bread together and eat cheese (and eat cheese).
Let us bake bread together and eat cheese (and eat cheese).
When I put it in the oven ready for a nice hot bun,
Oh lord, have mercy on me!

Let us make dread together on our sprees (on our sprees).
Let us make dread together on our sprees (on our sprees).
When I go on my sprees and, oh, so wild do I run,
Oh lord, have mercy on me!

Let us wake the dead together, if you please (if you please).
Let us wake the dead together, if you please (if you please).
When I go out and raise hell like Attila the Hun,
Oh lord, have mercy on me!

Original Words: Traditional spiritual

---

*Is it more probable that nature should go out of her course or that a man should tell a lie? We have never seen, in our time, nature go out of her course. But we have good reason to believe that millions of lies have been told in the same time. It is therefore at least millions to one that the reporter of a miracle tells a lie.*    *-- Thomas Paine*

## Oh, Earth Ship Please Swing
(Tune: O Worship the King)

Oh, earth ship please swing down here from above
And gratefully sing with us and make love.
Our shield and defender, your ship will we praise
While we party hard and all hell do we raise.

Oh, earth ship please swing on down and say "Hi".
Come hang out a while. Oh, don't be so shy.
Oh, come and enjoy our hospitality.
Oh, come see how friendly and fun we can be.

Oh, earth ship please swing around and come back,
But just do not bring your religious crap.
We'd like to delight in your sweet company
As long as you don't insult our dignity.

Original Words: Robert Grant, 1833

## When the Saints Go Marching In

I am just a lonesome trav'ler enjoying my world of sin,
Awaiting for that grand procession when the saints go marching in.

All my folks have gone before me and bought many a dozen,
So that we'll have lots of ammo when the saints go marching in.

Come and join me in my antics. I just can't wait to begin.
We'll shriek and roll with laughter when the saints go marching in.

CHORUS:
Oh, when the saints go marching in, oh, when the saints go marching in,
Oh, I will have my rotten eggs ready when the saints go marching in.

Original Words: R. E. Winsett

# Part 3

## Songs for Some

Use caution if sharing with your Christian friends.

# There Is a Fountain Filled With Blood

There is a fountain filled with blood from all god's violence wild,
Such as when he sent that big flood, killing every man and child,
Killing every man and child, killing every man and child,
Such as when he sent that big flood, killing every man and child.

The children of Sodom, you see, were such a crude, vile lot
That god just had to violently kill them in his evil plot,
Kill them in his evil plot, kill them in his evil plot,
That god just had to violently kill them in his evil plot.

He hardened Pharaoh's heart, so he refused to let Israel leave,
Then killed one of each family to cause mothers to grieve,
To cause mothers to grieve, to cause mothers to grieve,
Then killed one of each family to cause mothers to grieve.

He spread the sea so his folks could pass, then held it back until
The Egyptians entered in en masse. Then he drowned them for a thrill,
Then he drowned them for a thrill, he drowned them for a thrill.
The Egyptians entered in en masse. Then he drowned them for a thrill.

When Korah challenged Moses' hand our god just had a fit.
While with their wives and kids they did stand god killed them in a snit,
God killed them in a snit, god killed them in a snit.
While with their wives and kids they did stand god killed them in a snit.

Oh, fourteen thousand men he killed because they did speak out.
With graves the wilderness he filled of those who dared to doubt,
Of those who dared to doubt, of those who dared to doubt.
With graves the wilderness he filled of those who dared to doubt.

David numbered the Israelites, which made god mighty mad,
So seventy thousand god did smite who had done nothing bad,
Who had done nothing bad, who had done nothing bad.
So seventy thousand god did smite who had done nothing bad.

When David had Uriah killed and his sexy wife defiled
Then god acted with grace and skill and killed the innocent child,
And killed the innocent child, and killed the innocent child.
Then god acted with grace and skill and killed the innocent child,

The men of Bethshemesh did dare god's ark to look inside.
Then god exerted justice fair and fifty thousand died,
And fifty thousand died, and fifty thousand died.
Then god exerted justice fair and fifty thousand died.

God sent his folks to Canaan fair to kill them everyone,
Not a man or child to spare. Your conscience does this stun?
Your conscience does this stun? Your conscience does this stun?
Not a man or child to spare. Your conscience does this stun?

There is a fountain filled with blood from god's great murderous rule,
And if you trust in such a dud you'll truly be a fool,
You'll truly be a fool, you'll truly be a fool.
And if you trust in such a dud you'll truly be a fool.

Original Words: William Cowper, 1772

## When I See the Blood

*And when the LORD thy God shall deliver them before thee; thou shalt smite them, and utterly destroy them; thou shalt make no covenant with them, nor shew mercy unto them. -- Deut.7:2*

God sent his people to Canaan so grand
To kill all the people and steal their land.
"Kill them," god said, "to fulfill my great plan,
And I'll be, oh, so happy with you."

Hittites, Hivites and mean Girgishites --
Vile, evil people god wants you to smite.
"Rush in," god says, "and just treat them with spite,
And I'll be, oh, so happy with you."

Kill them all off and steal all they own --
Fields they have planted, trees they have grown.
"Kill them," god says, "with spears or with stones,
And I'll be, oh, so happy with you."

Kill every man, woman, daughter and son.
Strike them all down, and leave not a one.
"Gore them," god says, "it will be lots of fun,
And I'll be, oh, so happy with you."

CHORUS:
"When I see the blood, lots of nice, red blood,
When I see the blood  I'll be happy, so happy with you."

Original Words: John G. Foote, Elisha A. Hoffman

## On Jordan's Stormy Banks I Stand

On Jordan's stormy banks I stand and cast a wishful eye
To Canaan's fair and happy land where they are about to die.

God sends us in to Canaan's land to kill them every one,
To have an orgy of death so grand. It will be so much fun.

We'll kill them every man and woman, every child also,
And every baby god has damned. Oh, down to hell they'll go!

CHORUS:
I am bound for the promised land. We will make such a slaughter grand.
Oh, who will come and kill with me? I am bound for the promised land.

Original Words: Samuel Stennett, 1787

## God of War, Lead Onward
### (Tune: Cross of Christ, Lead Onward)

God has promised Israel a beautiful homeland
Filled with milk and honey -- such a place so grand.
There is just one problem; it's already filled,
But god has solved this problem. He'll just have them killed.

Girgashites and Hittites, and Canaanites, too.
Perizites and Jebusites, we're coming for you.
Amorites and Hivites, you won't get away
From our swords and arrows. We'll have a time so gay.

You chose the wrong real estate on which to build your lives.
God says we now own it, so you have to die.
We'd love to have you stay, but god just says, "No way."
You'd corrupt our morals, so all of you we'll slay.

So we come with god's love killing as we smile
Every man and woman, every dog and child.
Please know it's with love. The god of love we serve
Sends us to show his grace. From his plan we can't swerve.

CHORUS:
God of war, lead onward to the promised land.
We will kill everyone just as you command.

Original Words: Russell Kelso Carter

## Beneath the Cross of the Serpent
### (Tune: Beneath the Cross of Jesus)

*And the LORD sent fiery serpents among the people, and they bit the people; and much people of Israel died. And the LORD said unto Moses, Make thee a fiery serpent, and set it upon a pole: and it shall come to pass, that every one that is bitten, when he looketh upon it, shall live. -- Numbers 21:6,8*

Beneath the cross of the serpent, there I will take my stand
To heal me of the bite of snakes that god sent on the land.
Do not complain about the food or god gets plenty mad.
He'll send upon you ugly snakes. He can be a mean old dad.

Beneath the cross of the serpent, there I stand horrified.
Because god got into a snit see how many have died.
Oh, this is how he shows his love, that if you state your mind
He'll send on you a horror real or kill you. He's so kind.

Beneath the cross of the serpent, there I lift up my eyes.
The graven image now set up that Moses did devise.
No graven image we were told would our god tolerate,
But now we're told to look to it to save us from our fate.

Beneath the cross of the serpent I'm proud to take my place.
The serpent is a wise old beast -- gift to the human race.
In Eden he opened their eyes, so they could understand.
He broke them from god's evil snare their knowledge to expand.

Original Words: Elizabeth C. Clephane, 1868

## The God of Abraham Praise

*I am the God of Abraham thy father. -- Genesis 26:24*

The god of Abraham praise, who made him take his son,
Put him on an altar to slay for god's will to be done.
To our great god above the little ones belong.
Oh, don't you think that in this picture something is surely wrong?

The god of Abraham praise, who made his nation true
From the one who forced his slave to have sex and then threw
Her out when she had child to fend all on her own.
The hero upon whom god smiled.  It's enough to make you groan.

The god of Abraham praise. He threatened the king's life,
Because our great hero so brave did lie about his wife,
Then rewarded Abraham with lots of goods and slaves.
Oh, doesn't it make you so proud of how our god behaves?

Original Words: Daniel ben Judah (attrib.); Thomas Olivers, 1770

## Onward Christian Soldiers

Onward Christian soldiers marching out to war.
On the nonbelievers all our wrath we'll pour.
Those of other beliefs hear our fateful roar.
For those who do not believe us god's wrath is in store.

Onward Christian soldiers marching in god's will.
In the name of Jesus lots of blood we'll spill.
Crusades to the holy land. Muslims we will kill.
Kill all who will not convert. God's will we will fulfill.

Onward Christian soldiers marching as we go,
Killing infidels and witches blow by blow.
Hindus, Muslims, infidels each one is our foe.
Atheists and heretics all will reap our woe.

Onward Christian soldiers, how the earth will quake.
Catholics battle Protestants all for Jesus' sake.
Wars of faith we cherish, killing off the fakes.
Those with faulty doctrine we will burn at the stake.

CHORUS:
Onward Christian soldiers, marching out to war.
On the nonbelievers all our wrath we'll pour.

Original Words: S. Baring-Gould

## He Is So Willing
### (Tune: He Was Not Willing)

*The Lord ... is ... not willing that any should perish. -- 2 Peter 3:9*
*[A]ll these things are done in parables, [t]hat seeing they may see, and not perceive; and hearing they may hear, and not understand; lest at any time they should be converted, and their sins should be forgiven them. -- Mark 4:11-12*

He is so willing that many should perish.
Jesus enthroned in the glory above
Sees our poor fallen world, all of our sorrows;
Does not a damn thing, the great god of love.
Perishing! Perishing! Thronging our pathway,
Hearts break with burdens too heavy to bear.
Jesus does nothing to reach out or help them,
Nothing to lift them from sin and despair.

He is so willing that many should perish.
Leaves us to deal with our sorrow and pain.
He could come on down to help and to comfort,
But he just hides from us. Oh, what a shame!
Perishing! Perishing! What does he care?
No matter what happens he never draws near.
No matter how many die in their sins
Not once will they see him. His voice they won't hear.

He is so willing that many should perish.
Gave us two ears, a mouth, nose and two eyes.
Five senses he gave for us to perceive,
But show himself to us through them he denies.
Perishing! Perishing! Yet does he hide.
He never allows us to hear, touch or see.
Just keeps his wondrous love all to himself
While millions stream to hell continuously.

Original Words: Lucy Rider Meyer

## His Eye Is on the Sparrow

*Are not two sparrows sold for a farthing? and one of them shall not fall on the ground without your Father. -- Matthew 10:29*

Why do I feel discouraged? Why do the shadows come?
Why should my heart be lonely and wish for a nice chum?
'Cause Jesus is my portion. A big false hope is he.
His eye is on the sparrow, and that is how he treats me.
His eye is on the sparrow, and that is how he treats me.

Most sparrows die in childhood when they are young and weak.
Their outlook when they're born is really sad and bleak.
Now, Jesus cares for sparrows the Bible tells us to see.
His eye is on the sparrow, and that is how he treats me.
His eye is on the sparrow, and that is how he treats me.

The few who do survive to grow to maturity
Have parasites and diseases in multiplicity.
Now, Jesus is my buddy. He takes right care of me.
His eye is on the sparrow, and that is how he treats me.
His eye is on the sparrow, and that is how he treats me.

Every year that passes half of their flock does die
From predators and dangers -- enough to make you cry.
As Jesus sits in heaven and watches so tenderly
His eye is on the sparrow, and that is how he treats me.
His eye is on the sparrow, and that is how he treats me.

CHORUS:
I sing because I'm happy. (I'm happy.) I sing so stupidly. (Stupidly)
For his eye is on the sparrow, and that is how he treats me.

Original Words: Civilla D. Martin, 1905

> In the past 10,000 years, humans have devised roughly 100,000 religions based on roughly 2,500 gods. So the only difference between myself and the believers is that I am skeptical of 2,500 gods whereas they are skeptical of 2,499 gods. We're only one God away from total agreement.
> -- Michael Shermer

## They're Passing to Their Doom
### (Tune: A Missionary Cry)

A hundred thousand souls a day are passing one by one away
In Christless guilt and gloom.
Without one ray of hope or light, while Jesus just hides from their sight,
They're passing to their doom, they're passing to their doom.

Oh, holy god, why don't you move off from your ass and try to prove
That you're not cruel and cold.
Oh, try to show them some goodwill, rather than just to smite and kill,
As in the days of old, as in the days of old.

The god of mercy just sits back and hides his face to show he lacks
Of any love or care.
Just sends them all to burn in hell, makes not a damned effort to tell
Them that he's really there, oh, that he's really there.

CHORUS:
They're passing, passing fast away in thousands day by day.
They're passing to their doom. They're passing to their doom.

Original Words: A. B. Simpson

## Queerer, Still Queerer
(Tune: Nearer, Still Nearer)

Queerer, still queerer, I say from my heart.
Many are queer, but queerer thou art
Than any strange thing in earth or in sky.
You are so queer you all reason defy.
You are so queer you all reason defy.

Queerer, still queerer, nothing I bring.
Queerer than you I just can't find a thing.
Even my strange and devious heart
Could think of not a thing queerer to impart,
Could think of not a thing queerer to impart.

Queerer, still queerer, queerness is thine.
Hatefulness, too, when folks to hell you consign,
When they don't trust your love and your grace
While you stay distant and hide from them your face,
While you stay distant and hide from them your face.

Original Words: Mrs. C. H. Morris

## Queerer, My God, Art Thee
(Tune: Nearer, My God, To Thee)

Queerer, my god, art thee. Queerer art thee.
I get a nice big laugh at such lunacy.
This all my song shall be: "Queerer, my god, art thee.
Queerer, my god, art thee! Queerer art thee!"

You created all things that ever lived.
Most have just died away. A poor job you did.
So all my song shall be: "Queerer, my god, art thee.
Queerer, my god, art thee! Queerer art thee!"

You made a body fine for me to dwell.
Appendix you installed to serve me so well.
So all my song shall be: "Queerer, my god, art thee.
Queerer, my god, art thee! Queerer art thee!"

You gave me hearing, sight, taste, smell and touch,
Then hide from my senses five. You love me so much.
One thing is plain to see: "Queerer, my god, art thee.
Queerer, my god, art thee! Queerer art thee!"

You told your people fine, "Thou shalt not kill,"
Then sent them to Canaan their blood to spill.
So all my song shall be: "Queerer, my god, art thee.
Queerer, my god, art thee! Queerer art thee!"

You gave your servant Job to Satan and let
Him kill his family, torture him to win a bet.
So all my song shall be: "Queerer, my god, art thee.
Queerer, my god, art thee! Queerer art thee!"

David you hurt not when he disobeyed your will.
Seventy thousand innocent people you killed.
So all my song shall be: "Queerer, my god, art thee.
Queerer, my god, art thee! Queerer art thee!"

Jacob lied and cheated, stole from his brother dear.
You blessed him for his evil deeds. You really are so queer.
So all my song shall be: "Queerer, my god, art thee.
Queerer, my god, art thee! Queerer art thee!"

Original Words: H. D. Ganse; Author: Sarah Flower Adams (1841)

> *There is not enough love and kindness in the world to give any of it away to imaginary beings.*
> *-- Friederich Nietzsche*

## Jesus Loves the Little Children

Jesus loves the little children, all the children of the world.
That is why they pass away from hunger every day.
Jesus loves the little children of the world.

Jesus loves the little children, all the children of the world.
That is why Elisha called some bears the kids to maul.
Jesus loves the little children of the world.

Jesus loves the little children, all the children of the world.
That is why he does nothing while abusers have their fling.
Jesus loves the little children of the world.

More verses:
… That's why he burned them up in Sodom so corrupt…
… That's why he sent the flood to drown them in the mud…
… That's why he counts the sins of the fathers on their kids…
… That's why he sends disease to give them a little tease…

Original Words: C. H. Woolston

> *When one person suffers from a delusion, it is called insanity. When many people suffer from a delusion it is called a Religion.* --Robert M. Pirsig

## God Moves in a Mysterious Way

God moves in a mysterious way his wonders to perform.
He sends us famines, floods and droughts and kills us in his storms.

Tornados, blizzards, hurricanes he creates with deadly skill
To freeze, destroy and cause suff'ring, and many folks to kill.

Oh, deadly organisms created by god above
That make us sick and kill us off remind us of his love.

Yes, tidal waves and earthquakes, too, against our lands are hurled.
Volcanoes spit their fiery wrath upon his precious world.

The god of nature has, they say, control of everything.
Omnipotent they say he is, and this is what he brings.

Yes, my friend, how true it is, he is mysterious.
He sends us all these wondrous things to show his love to us.

Original Words: Wm. Cowper, 1774

## God Is a Snare To You
(Tune: God Will Take Care of You)

Trust not in god whate'er betide. God is a snare to you.
Don't let religion take you for a ride. God is a snare to you.
[Chorus] God is a snare to you thru every day, o'er all the way.
Don't stuff your brain in your shoe. God is a snare to you.

Don't base your life on tales and myths. God is a snare to you.
Or spend your short life in ignorance bliss. God is a snare to you.
[Chorus] God is a snare to you thru every day, o'er all the way.
Don't let your brain turn to goo. God is a snare to you.

To believe in god will mess up your mind. God is a snare to you.
Do not keep your brain in your behind. God is a snare to you.
[Chorus] God is a snare to you thru every day, o'er all the way.
Don't believe nonsense untrue. God is a snare to you.

Original Words: Cevilla D. Martin, 1904

## Guide Me Not, Thou Great Big Jokester
(Tune: Guide Me, O Thou Great Jehovah)

Guide me not, thou great big jokester. Pilgrim through this barren land.
I am weak, but thou art tricky. Watch out for your sleight of hand.
Dread of heaven, dread of heaven, go away I want no more (want no more).
Go away I want no more.

Guide me not, thou great big jokester. Life's already hard enough.
I don't mean to be rude, but I really just don't need your guff.
Troll of heaven, troll of heaven, don't go off in a big huff (a big huff).
Don't go off in a big huff.

Original Words: William Williams (1745); Peter Williams (1771, translator)

## What a Friend We Have in Jesus

What a friend we have in Jesus, like a big old teddy bear,
And he's just as helpful as one when you come to god in prayer!
Oh, what peace we often forfeit. Oh, what needless pain we bear,
When we insist on believing god will listen to our prayer.

Have we trials and afflictions? Is there trouble anywhere?
If you'd like a good placebo take it to the lord in prayer.
If you wish to blabber on and speak into the empty air,
Fantasizing someone hears you, take it to the lord in prayer.

Are you weak and heavy laden, cumbered with a load of care?
If you'd like to keep that feeling take it to the lord in prayer.
Do thy friends despise, forsake thee? Do they just not seem to care?
Add just one more to that list and take it to the lord in prayer.

Blessed savior, he has promised all our burdens he would bear
If we were to come and bring them to our lord in earnest prayer.
But when we get down to pray, our problems with Jesus to share,
Talk with him for a few moments, we find that he's just not there.

Original Words: Joseph Medlicott Scriven, 1855

## Imaginary Friend Is Jesus
### (Tune: What a Friend We Have in Jesus)

(Im-)aginary friend is Jesus. I talk to him everywhere.
I imagine that I carry everything to god in prayer.
Oh, what peace it makes me feel. Makes me giddy, I declare.
Gives me such a pleasant feeling fantasizing he is there.

(Im-)aginary friend is Jesus. He goes with me everywhere.
Right inside my head he lives to help me with my every care.
He is such a friend so faithful. All my life I with him share.
Never do I let it phase me that he isn't really there.

(Im-)aginary friend is Jesus, no matter what folks declare.
They're just jealous because I've a friend of whom they're not aware.
They'd like to take away my friend, leave me in a great despair,
But I won't give up my Jesus just because he is not there.

Original Words: Joseph Medlicott Scriven, 1855

## Keep in Touch With Jesus

Would you be a victor over every foe --
Knock them down, beat them up, make them eat crow?
Jesus Christ can teach you how their bones to crunch.
Keep in touch with Jesus. He'll thank you a bunch.

Would you be a blessing each and every day
To those who will agree to see it your way?
The rest of them are losers. They're just out to lunch.
Keep in touch with Jesus. He'll thank you a bunch.

Would you have communion with your lord each day,
Listen to the silly things he has to say?
He would like to meet up with you to have brunch.
Keep in touch with Jesus. He'll thank you a bunch.

CHORUS:
Keep in touch with Jesus. Bring to him a grin.
He just gets so lonely when you don't call in.
Keep up your long distance. Pay your bill each month.
Keep in touch with Jesus. He'll thank you a bunch.

Original Words: C. S. Kauffrman

## The Lily of the Valley

I have found a friend in Jesus, such a nice fantasy!
He's the best imaginary friend around.
The Lily of the Valley, as cute as a sweet pea.
And as soft and loveable as a blood hound.
In sorrow you can't find him. In trouble he won't stay,
But that's alright 'cause I am on a roll.

He all my sense has taken -- left me like an acorn.
In temptation he's my strong and mighty flower.
I've all for him forsaken, except for a little porn.
Now all his silly notions I devour.
Though all the world forsake me and Satan tempt me sore,
Just to plant more pretty lilies is my goal.

He will never, never leave me, nor yet forsake me here,
While I live by faith, with nonsense my head fill.
A wall of fire about me, I've nothing now to fear.
I just use it now my hamburgers to grill.
Then when I'm picking lilies and see his blessed face,
I will lay down and I'll do a belly roll.

CHORUS:
He's the Lily of the Valley, smooth as a banana peel.
Just don't step on him when you walk out through the field.

Original Words: Charles W. Frye, 1881

## The Cavalry
(Tune: At Calvary)

Years ago I learned that Jesus died. When they told how he was crucified
I listened hoping that in would ride the cavalry.

By god's word the story I first learned, how that sweet little Jesus they spurned.
Hoped to hear that in time in had churned the cavalry.

Now, I've tried to think of everything that they might have done to save my king,
Wishing that it had been they did bring the cavalry.

CHORUS:
Poor old Jesus hanging on a tree. Will somebody listen to his plea?
Who can we find to come set him free? The cavalry!

Original Words: William R. Newell, 1895

## In the Hour of Trial

In the hour of trial, Jesus, plead for me.
Make sure my denial ends in victory.
When you see me waver give the judge a bribe,
So he'll find in my favor and give me good vibes.

In the hour of trial I'll claim innocence.
The devil, oh so vile, made me lose my sense.
Jesus, come and save me. Guilty I won't plea.
Jesus will so brave be, get me off scot-free.

In the hour of trial the judge sure looks mean.
What can make him smile so to "innocent" he'll lean?
Jesus, you can do it. I have seen your tricks before.
If you'll just get to it you'll get me out the door.

Original Words: James Montgomery, 1834

## Pass the Pot
(Tune: Pass Me Not)

Pass the pot, oh gentle savior. Hear my humble cry.
While with others thou art toking, do not pass me by.

Pass the pot, oh gentle savior. Give me sweet relief.
Let's enjoy a little high from that marijuana leaf.

Pass the pot, oh gentle savior. Share your nice pure weed.
Make me feel right light and happy. Set my spirit free.

CHORUS:
Savior, savior, hear my humble cry.
While with others thou art toking, do not pass me by.

Original Words: Fanny Crosby, 1868

## Wily Schemer
(Tune: My Redeemer)

I will sing of a wily schemer. How wily he is to me.
I know of no one any meaner than Jesus Christ, the enemy.

He sure is a wily schemer. Just loves his tricks to play.
But he's as cute as a little lemur, so I just laugh at him each day.

Jesus Christ, the wily schemer, what a wily pest is he.
Wants to put my brain in his steamer, turn up the heat 'til I'm dumb as a flea.

CHORUS:
Sing, oh, sing, the wily schemer, Oh, how wily he is to me.
He's a wily little dreamer. Thinks he's going to get me!

Original Words: Philip P. Bliss, 1876

## I Would Be Like Jesus

Earthly pleasures vainly call me. I would be like Jesus.
Rather have people extoll me. I would be like Jesus.

People thinking I'm a god. I would be like Jesus.
When in truth I'm just a fraud. Oh, I would be like Jesus.

Just to have folks give me glory. I would be like Jesus.
When I tell a stupid story. I would be like Jesus.

Tell people I'm high and mighty. I would be like Jesus.
When I am just really flighty. I would be like Jesus.

CHORUS:
Be like Jesus, this my song. Have folks follow me along
If I'm right or I am wrong. I would be like Jesus.

Original Words: James Rowe

## Calling Today

Jesus is tenderly calling your phone. Calling today, calling today.
Pick up and listen so on he can drone and drone and drone away.

Jesus, I wish you would give it a rest. Calling today, calling today.
Calling so often you're just such a pest. Someone take his phone away.

Jesus is calling to bother me now. Calling today, calling today.
I wish he would go and pester some cow and let me get on with my day.

CHORUS:
Calling today, calling today, Jesus is calling, oh, calling to drone away.

Original Words: Fanny Crosby

# Somebody's Knocking at Your Door

Somebody's knocking at your door. Somebody's knocking at your door.
Oh, sinner, why don't you tell him to go pester the likes of Thor?
(1.)Knocks like Jesus. Somebody's knocking at your door.
(1.)Knocks like Jesus. It's probably someone you abhor.
Oh, sinner, why don't you tell him to go away and pester Thor?

(2.)Can't you hear him?
(3.)Answer Jesus.

Original Words: African-American spiritual

# He's Just Not of the Flip-Flopping Kind
(Tune: Are You Washed in the Blood?)
And it repented the Lord that he had made man on the earth. -- Genesis 6:6

God made the heavens and the earth and plants and the animals and the sea.
He made mankind in his own image and declared it so good to be.

Then after a while he changed his mind, and was sorry he'd made a mistake.
Seeing how he had screwed it all up he washed away all he did make.

A great big flood that covered the earth he sent from heaven above
To kill every woman, man and child, and thus demonstrated his love.

After he killed everything on earth he was sorry for what he had sent.
"Oh, never will I do that again. I need better anger management."

CHORUS:
God's word says god's not man that he should change his mind.
It's so good to know that you can trust in god.
He's just not of the flip-flopping kind.

Original Words: Elisha A. Hoffman, 1878

# In the Garden

I come to the garden alone while the dew is still on the roses.
Then, as I fear, I fall on my ear when I trip on one of the hoses.

He speaks, and the sound of his voice is so shrill the birds hush their singing.
And the headache free that he gave to me within my head is ringing.

I'd stay in the garden with him until my strength comes back to me,
But he runs away ere him back I can pay. He really knows how to screw me.

CHORUS:
And he gawks at me and throws rocks at me, and he laughs at me as I groan.
And then he will stare as I cuss and swear, then hit me with one final stone.

Original Words: C. Austin Miles, 1913

# Thunder-Filled, Blunder-Filled Jesus
(Tune: Wonderful, Wonderful Jesus)

There is never a day so dreary. There is never a night so long,
But the soul that is looking at Jesus will see he resembles King Kong.

He thunders and blunders so heavy, trying to create lots of woe.
He just tries to look, oh, so scary while putting on his big show.

But we know that his thunder is empty -- just full of hot air that he blows.
He just looks, oh, so pitifully foolish each time a new tantrum he throws.

His blunders, they are so many it is hard to keep track of them all.
It is dizzying when we remember his blunders both big and small.

CHORUS:
Thunder-filled, blunder-filled Jesus, to him we now offer this song:
How stupid and foolish and silly he looks when he thunders and blunders all wrong.

Original Words: Anna B. Russell

> Faith: Not wanting to know what is true.
> -- Friedrich Nietzsche

# Safe from the Harms of Jesus
(Tune: Safe in the Arms of Jesus)

Safe from the harms of Jesus, far from that miserable pest.
Away from his stupid nonsense finally my soul can rest.
No more to talk of angels and other stupidity.
From such ridiculous hoodoo now I am finally free.

Safe from the harms of Jesus, no more he overbears.
Enjoying the world's temptations, no more he does me scare.
No more he causes sorrow, no more the doubts and fears.
Now I've come to my senses. No more he brings me tears.

Safe from the harms of Jesus, I use my brain again.
No longer do I babble and squawk like a damn old hen.
Now I finally move forward, make something of my life,
Rather than spending my days babbling like Barney Fife.

CHORUS:
Safe from the harms of Jesus, far from that awful pest,
Far from his stupid nonsense, finally my soul can rest.

Original Words: Fanny Crosby, 1868

## Count Your Dressings
### (Tune: Count Your Blessings)

When upon life's billows you are tempest tossed,
When you are discouraged, thinking all is lost,
Count your many dressings, name them one by one,
And it will surprise you what harm god has done.

Are you ever burdened with a load of care,
Because Jesus treated you mean and unfair?
Count your many dressings, every doubt will fly.
You will know for sure he's just an awful guy.

When you look at others with their lands and gold,
Wonder why god from you does that stuff withhold,
Count your many dressings – you will realize
The wounds that god has given money doesn't buy.

CHORUS:
Count your dressings. Name them one by one.
Count your dressings. See what god has done!
Count your dressings, head down to your bum.
Count your many dressings. See what god hath done!

Original Words: Johnson Oatman, 1897

## Torment by Torment
### (Tune: Moment by Moment)

Trying is Jesus, that savior of mine.
Whatever I ask for he'll surely decline.
Just causes trouble and treats me like swine.
Torment by torment, lord, torments are thine.

Lying is Jesus, the master of spin.
Said he would help me and save me from sin.
Instead, he loves to make me curse and whine.
Torment by torment, lord, torments are thine.

Crying to Jesus -- it just does no good.
Might as well talk to a statue of wood.
Thinking about him sends chills up my spine.
Torment by torment, lord, torments are thine.

CHORUSL
Torment by torment he shows me his love.
Torment by torment he smites from above.
Looking to Jesus who treats us like swine.
Torment by torment, lord, torments are thine.

Original Words: D. W. Whittle

## I Am Wary Just to Walk With Him
### (Tune: It Is Glory Just to Walk With Him)

I am wary just to walk with him because he's so tricky.
It is danger for my soul each day.
You never know when he will push or suddenly trip me.
Oh, my god! I'm wary all the way.

I am wary when the shadows fall to know that he is near,
Just because on me he likes to prey.
I am wary to abide in him when skies above are clear.
Yes, with him I'm wary all the way.

I am wary when I walk with him with heaven's holy crowd,
Just to pass on through that big, wild fray,
For fear that he will throw me off the edge of some damn cloud
To fall to earth all the way.

CHORUS:
I am wary just to walk with him.
I am wary just to walk with him.
He keeps me all affright through the vale and o'er the height.
I am wary just to walk with him.

Original Words: Alvis B. Christiansen

## How Obscene
### (Tune: I'm Redeemed)

I can sing now the song how religion's all wrong.
Oh, it's such a ridiculous sham.
I am free from all doubt, and I join in the shout,
"How obscene is the crud of this scam!"

Oh, I know it's all jive, crock of bull. Man alive!
How they preach such malarkey goddamned.
Are they just not so bright? Are they missing a light?
How obscene is the crud of this scam!

It's disgrace every day. I'm appalled by the way
Up your ass their nonsense they do cram.
All their fables and myths, won't they jump off a cliff!
How obscene is the crud of this scam!

CHORUS:
How obscene! How obscene!
Jesus' myth is a scam so obscene. Don't let 'em screw ya!
And I join with the throng that from this madness does scram.
"How obscene is the crud of this scam!"

Original Words: Russell Kelso Carter

## Queer the Cross
(Tune: Near the Cross)

Jesus died upon a cross -- a Roman execution.
Somehow that's supposed to give our sins absolution.

Adam ate from the wrong tree. God damned us from spite,
But then he sent his son to die. That made everything alright.

Jesus died upon a cross. That's the story they tell.
If you buy that load of crock you won't go to hell.

Jesus died for you and me, if you believe this crap,
But rose again in three short days, so it was just a long nap.

CHORUS:
Queer the cross! Queer the cross! What a strange idea
That dying on a cross should save us from our sins. How queer!

Original Words: Fanny Crosby, 1869

## Only Believe

Only believe the tale that I weave. Though it's not plausible, only believe.

Only believe what's up my sleeve. I'll feed you lots of bull. Only believe!

Original Words: Paul Rader, 1921

## Whosoever Will

"Whosoever heareth," shout, shout the sound!
Spread the blessed tidings all the world around.
Spread the joyful joke wherever man is found:
Whosoever will may come.

Whosoever cometh do not delay.
We're ready to hoodwink, fool you while we may.
Come and our sweet Jesus will on you jokes play.
Whosoever will may come.

Whosoever falleth for our line of crock,
We'll give him some myths his intelligence to block.
Then we'll pull his ears 'til he looks like Mr. Spok.
Whosoever will may come.

CHORUS:
Whosoever will, whosoever will,
Anyone who's fool enough to swallow this swill.
'Tis a loving father wants to keep you dumb.
Whosoever will may come.

Original Words: P. P. Bliss, 1870

## Blunder-Filled Words of Lies
(Tune: Wonderful Words of Life)

Sing them over again to me, blunder-filled words of lies.
Let me more of their blunders see, blunder-filled words of lies.
Words so stupid and crazy. Never cease to amaze me.

Christ, the crazy one, gives to all blunder-filled words of lies.
If you're silly then you might fall for blunder-filled words of lies.
All so freely given, into our fool heads driven.

Words that issue the gospel's call, blunder-filled words of lies.
Myths fantastic and tales so tall, blunder-filled words of lies.
Jesus, only savior, gives you good behavior.

CHORUS:
Whimsical words, fanciful words, blunder-filled words of lies.
Comical words, laughable words, blunder-filled words of lies.

Original Words: P. P. Bliss, 1874

## Stranded on the Promises
(Tune: Standing on the Promises)

Stranded on the promises of Christ my king.
All that damned malarkey didn't mean a thing.
And so now has ended my religious fling.
Stranded on the promises of god.

Stranded on the promises that did me fail,
Oh, how my intelligence they did assail.
Maybe now some sense and reason can prevail.
Stranded on the promises of god.

Stranded on the promises I now can see
What a mess of crock and bull they came to be.
From their lies and madness I long to be free.
Stranded on the promises of god.

Stranded on the promises of Christ the lord.
All my supplications he has sure ignored.
No longer this foolishness I can afford.
Stranded on the promises of god.

Stranded on the promises I cannot fall,
Because I am already let down by them all.
No longer will I believe the tales so tall.
Stranded on the promises of god.

CHORUS:
Stranded, stranded, stranded on the promises of god. Oh, Jesus!
Stranded, stranded, I'm stranded on the promises of god.

Original Words: Russell Kelso Carter, 1886

# Once
### (Tune: Himself)

Once I trusted fairies. Now it is the lord.
Fairies were so charming. Now I am just bored.
Once I was creative. Now god's book I own.
Once I was such fun, but now leave me alone.

Once 'twas honest trying. Now 'tis mindless trust.
Once I used my head, but now my brain will rust.
Once 'twas busy planning. Now 'tis trustful prayer.
Once 'twas thoughtful caring. Now just cuss and swear.

Once I hoped in Jesus. Now I know he's mine.
Once I was so good, but now my ass does shine.
Once for death I waited. Now his coming hail.
Once I used my reason. Now think like a snail.

Once I used my brain, but now 'tis just blind faith.
Once I was so sane, and now believe in wraiths.
Once I used to try to think and understand.
Now the myths I buy. Keep my head in the sand.

CHORUS:
All in all forever, Jesus will I sing.
No more I'll think or reason. Just to his myths I'll cling.

Original Words: Albert Benjamin Simpson, c.1891

# Since I Have Been Deceived
### (Tune: Since I Have Been Redeemed)

I have a song I love to sing, since I have been deceived.
About that strange religious thing, since I have been deceived.

I have a Christ who satisfies, since I have been deceived.
By telling lots of downright lies, since I have been deceived.

I have a witness bright and clear, since I have been deceived.
Because it got shoved up my rear, since I have been deceived.

I have a home prepared for me, since I have been deceived.
At least, that is my fantasy, since I have been deceived.

I have a joy I can't express, since I have been deceived.
So what if my life is just a mess, since I have been deceived.

CHORUS:
Since I have been deceived,
Since I have been deceived I will swear with Jesus name.
Since I have been deceived I will cuss and swear with Jesus' name.

Original Words: E. O. Excell

## Leaning on the Never Lasting Arms
(Tune: Leaning on the Everlasting Arms)

What a crock of shit, what a great big lie, leaning on the never lasting arms.
What a cussed mess, what false hope is mine, leaning on the never lasting arms.

Oh, how sweet to live with head in the sand, leaning on the never lasting arms.
Enjoying each day in ignorant bliss so grand, leaning on the never lasting arms.

What have I to dread? What have I to fear, leaning on the never lasting arms?
I have never peace with my lord so queer, leaning on the never lasting arms.

CHORUS:
Leaning, leaning, trusting in all his magic charms.
Leaning, leaning, leaning on the never lasting arms.

Original Words: E. A. Hoffman, 1887

## Jesus, Jesus, Jesus
(Tune: He Keeps Me Singing)

There's within my heart a fantasy. Picks me up when I feel low.
Use imagination and I see Jesus everywhere I go.

Tried to use my marbles all my life, think and reason every day.
Then I put my faith in Jesus Christ. Now I let my brain decay.

Jesus is a fantasy so sweet, makes me want to sing and dance.
All his myths and fables are so neat, almost make me wet my pants.

CHORUS:
Jesus, Jesus, Jesus, what a crazy show.
Keeps me ever laughing. The more I hear the less I know.

Original Words: Luther B. Bridgers, 1910

## How Marvelous! How Wonderful!

I stand amazed in the presence of Jesus the Nazarene
And wonder have I lost my sense, this story is so obscene.

He took my sins and my sorrows. He made them his very own.
So now for all my tomorrows on and on his queer myth I'll drone.

When with the ransomed in glory his face I at last shall see,
I'll still be telling this story -- my wonderful fantasy.

CHORUS:
How marvelous! How wonderful! And my song shall ever be:
How marvelous! How wonderful is my savior fantasy.

Original Words: Charles Hutchinson Gabriel, 1905

# We're Starching Our Nylons
(Tune: We're Marching to Zion)

Come, we that love the lord, and bring our nylons out.
Those silky stockings so adored, we'll starch them up stiff as a board,
Oh, nice and firm and stout -- oh, nice and firm and stout.

Let those refuse to starch who never nylons wear,
But we who want to have a fling will get right on with our starching.
We'll starch them up with care. We'll starch them up with care.

Beliefs we have in god are like our nylons fair.
They've not a single factual base. We starch them up with our blind faith,
And fill our heads with air, and fill our heads with air.

CHORUS:
We're starching our nylons -- beautiful, beautiful nylons.
We're starching up our good nylons so we can look pretty for god.

Original Words: Isaac Watts

> *The whole religious complexion of the modern world is due to the absence from Jerusalem of a lunatic asylum.*        -- Thomas Paine

# Come, Hide With Me
(Tune: Abide With Me)

Come, hide with me. The world's a scary place.
Let's just pretend that there's a god of grace.
It's such relief to live in fantasy.
Won't you join in it and come hide with me?

Come, hide with me. The truth's a scary thing.
Rather to myths and fables let us cling.
Won't you come join me in my lunacy?
Escape from the real world and come hide with me.

Come, hide with me. Even though it be a fraud
It makes me feel good to pretend there's a god.
Please don't be put off by my insanity.
Just play along and come hide with me.

Come, hide with me. I can't face reality.
Imaginary friend for my malady.
It's better than dealing with truth, can't you see?
Give me religion, and come hide with me.

Original Words: Henry Francis Lyte, 1847

## Oh, Drug That Wilt Not Let Me Go
(Tune: O Love That Wilt Not Let Me Go)

Oh, drug that wilt not let me go, that's what religion is to me.
Oh, give me back my life you stole. No longer do I want to blow
My life on absurdity.

Oh, bug that so sickens my soul, that is what Jesus is to me.
Your lies have taken such a toll. My brain is like a lump of coal
When I listen to thee.

Oh, thug that my brain power stole, return my sanity to me.
Oh, give me back my life's control. Just don't be such an evil troll.
From your trap set me free.

Original Words: George Matheson, 1882

> *When the missionaries first came to Africa they had the Bible and we had the land. They said, "Let us pray." We closed our eyes. When we opened them we had the Bible and they had the land.*
> *-- Bishop Desmond Tutu*

## Singing in the Eaves
(Tune: Bringing in the Sheaves)

Singing in the morning. Singing songs of kindness.
Singing in the noontide and the dewy eve.
Singing in the harvest and the time of reaping.
We are dumb rejoicing, singing in the eaves.

Singing in the sunshine. Singing in the shadows.
Fearing neither clouds nor winter's chilling breeze.
Singing in the harvest with the labor ended.
We are dumb rejoicing, singing in the eaves.

Going forth with singing. Singing for the master.
Singing all his songs no matter who it peeves.
Sing over and over until we to hell come.
We are dumb rejoicing, singing in the eaves.

CHORUS:
Singing in the eaves. Singing in the eaves.
We are dumb rejoicing, singing in the eaves.
Singing in the eaves. Singing in the eaves.
We are dumb rejoicing, singing in the eaves.

Original Words: Knowles Shaw, 1874

# Read the Bible Every Day
### (Tune: Jesus, Loves Me, This I Know)

Read the Bible every day. To details attention pay.
Scrutinize its every word to see how it's so absurd.

Read the Bible; it's a gas. It will just tickle your ass
With all of its stories wild. You'll see why it's so reviled.

Read the Bible; it's so fun. Incredible stories are spun.
Thrilling stuff it has in store, especially if you love gore.

Read the Bible with open mind. Consider everything you find.
Use your brain to scrutinize before you accept its lies.

CHORUS:
Yes, read the Bible. You'll get an eyeful.
And if you buy bull the Bible's full of it.

Original Words: Anna Bartlett Warner, 1859; David Rutherford

# Holy Bible, Book Divine

Holy Bible, book divine, word of god, oh what a line!
Tries to tell me whence I came with a story that's so lame.

Holy Bible, book divine, like a hemorrhoid thou art mine.
Mine thou art to guide and guard and turn my brain into lard.

Holy Bible, book so fine if your brain's out on cloud nine.
Oh, thou holy book divine, perfect swill to feed to swine.

Original Words: John Burton, 1803

# Thy Word Is Like a Garden, Lord

Thy word is like a garden, lord, with weeds so strong and fair,
And everyone who seeks will find some stinging nettle there.
Thy word is like a deep, deep pit in which someone may fall,
And so get mired in all your shit, which sane minds does appall.

Thy word is like a garden, lord, with lots of kinds of fruit,
So filled with lots of worms and rot from the top down to the root.
Thy word is like a siren's call, so beautiful to hear,
Until you find your life shipwrecked, your days so glum and drear.

Thy word is like a garden, lord, with veggies of all kinds,
But when one tries to pick one it's full of disease he finds.
Thy word is like a deep, dark grave, all filled with rotting bones,
And anyone who ventures there with shock and horror groans.

Original Words: Edwin Hodder, 1863

## To the Regions Beyond

To the regions beyond I must go, I must go
Where the story has never been told.
To the millions that never have heard our tall tale
I must tell them our flimflam so bold (so bold).

To the hardest of places he calls me to go,
Never thinking of comfort or ease,
I must go and so eagerly fill up their heads
With our gobbledygook and our sleaze (our sleaze).

Oh now, you that are spending your leisure and powers
In efforts of reason and thought,
Forget all that crap and come join in our scam
To fill up all their heads with our rot (our rot).

CHORUS:
To the regions beyond I must go, I must go,
'Til the world, all the world, his malarkey shall know.

Original Words: Albert B. Simpson

## We've a Story to Tell to the Nations

We've a story to tell to the nations that shall make their faces blush bright.
A story fantastic, oh mercy! See if at our nonsense they'll bite.
See if at our nonsense they'll bite.

We've a story to tell to the nations that shall lift their spirit, oh lord!
They'll hear our fantastic concoctions. Our craftiness will be adored.
Our craftiness will be adored.

We've a story to tell to the nations that the lord who reigneth above
Hath sent us his son to save us from all the things that we love,
From all the things that we love.

CHORUS:
For the darkness shall turn to dawning, and the dawning to noonday bright.
The crazy story we're spawning will keep them laughing all the night.

Original Words: H. Ernest Nichol, 1896

## Go Ye Into All the World

Far, far away, in heathen lightness dwelling,
Millions of souls escaped our first onslaught.
Who, who will go, salvation's story telling,
Preaching our crap to fill their heads with snot?

See o'er the world wide-open doors inviting
Soldiers of Christ their wild stories to spin.
Christians, awake! Your forces all uniting.
If they won't believe you kick them in the shin.

God speed the day when those of every nation
With joy and gladness parodies shall sing.
Sinful, irreverent, rejoicing in temptation.
To Christians reality they will bring.

CHORUS:
All power is given unto me to fill their brains with idiocy.
Go ye into all the world and preach our nonsense,
And don't let them know you're a wussy.

Original Words: James McGranahan, 1886

## Faith Is the Trickery
(Tune: Faith Is the Victory)

Encamped along the hills of light, ye Christian soldiers rise
And press the battle so we can blight mankind with our lies.
Against the foe, those in the know, let all our strength be hurled.
Faith is the trickery, we know, that helps us fool the world.

On ev'ry hand the foe we find drawn up in dread array,
And armed with facts of every kind, and reason they display.
How shall we spread our faulty creed when facts our views belie?
We'll tell them faith is all they need. Then they'll believe our lie!

To him who overcomes the foe great kudos shall be giv'n.
We'll tell him that one day he'll go to a great place called heav'n.
No need to give him any basis showing it is true.
We'll just tell him to have some faith, and he'll believe our spew.

CHORUS:
Faith is the trickery! Faith is the trickery!
Oh, glorious trickery that helps us fool the world.

Original Words: John Henry Yates

## Sorry Be To Him Who Trusts Us
(Tune: Glory Be to Him Who Loved Us)

Sorry be to him who trusts us, trusts our ludicrous refrain.
By the time we finish messing with his mind he'll be insane.
Logic, good sense, reason and prudence from his head we'll surely drain.

"Sorry be to him who trusts us", so our choir triumphant sings.
Fables, myths and superstition to his mind our hogwash brings.
Baffle, schmoozle, dupe and bamboozle, fill his head with foolish things.

Sorry be to him who trusts us, joins our band of religious folks.
We'll bamboozle him completely. He won't realize on him's the joke.
Then we'll laugh. What a gaff!  See, he fell for our Jesus hoax!

Original Words: Horatius Bonar

## I Will Sing the Wondrous Story

I will sing the wondrous story of the Christ of fantasy-
An old tale of lies so sorry people treat me with pity.

I was lost, but Jesus found me; at least, that's the tale I tell.
That old myth did so astound me I just had to give 'em hell.

I am happy as I go on spreading myths and tales so wild.
While the lies and fibs just flow on I'll laugh like a little child.

CHORUS:
Yes, I'll sing the wondrous story of the Christ of fantasy.
Sing it with the saints so sorry and then laugh hysterically.

Original Words: Francis H. Rowley, 1886

## When I Purvey the Blunderous Dross
(Tune: When I Survey the Wondrous Cross)

When I purvey the blunderous dross of how the prince of glory died,
I find myself at such a loss to know how my lies folks will abide.

Forbid it, lord, that I should boast how o'er their eyes I pull the wool.
All the naïve minds amaze me the most that will accept such crock and bull.

Were the whole realm of nature mine, that were a resource far too small.
I still could never create or design such an incredible tale so tall.

Original Words: Isaac Watts, 1707

## Rescue the Perishing

Rescue the perishing. Care for the dying.
Snatch them in pity from religion's grip.
Weep o'er the erring one. Just keep on trying
To save poor folks from religion's bad trip.

Rescue the perishing. Duty demands it.
No more let religion wreck people's lives.
Rescue the perishing while god on his hands sits.
Snatch them from religion which sense deprives.

Rescue the perishing. God will not do it.
Just sends earthquakes and tornados to kill.
Just writes a book filled with lots of untrue shit.
Won't show his face. Sends us to hell to grill.

CHORUS:
Rescue the perishing. Care for the dying. Help them not be to religion a slave.

Original Words: Fanny Crosby, 1869

## Scour Out the Crud
(Tune: There Is Power in the Blood)

Would you be free from your burden of dirt?
Then scour out the crud! Scour out the crud!
Would you o'er dirt and grime success assert?
Then get in and scour out the crud!

Would you be free from your intelligence drain?
Then scour out the crud! Scour out the crud!
Get rid of myths and superstition from your brain.
Oh, get in and scour out the crud!

Would you be free to live true to your heart?
Then scour out the crud! Scour out the crud!
With senseless religion then have not a part.
Oh, get in and scour out the crud!

CHORUS:
Come and scour, scour, roll up those sleeves and scour
Out the crud of the lamb!
Come and scour, scour, roll up those sleeves and scour
Out that blasted crud of the lamb!

Original Words: Lewis E. Jones, 1899

## No Longer Will I Squander
(Tune: When the Roll Is Called Up Yonder)

When the trumpet of the lord shall sound and play a happy song,
Then I'll pick for him a nice and pretty flower,
But until he shows up with all his angels tagging along,
No longer will I squander my brain power.

On that bright and cloudless morning when the dead in Christ shall rise
And will take a nice and warm refreshing shower,
Then I'll put my trust in Jesus, but until I see his eyes
No longer will I squander my brain power.

When I have some reason to believe the foolishness they spew,
Then all of his crazy teachings I'll devour,
But as long as they just babble like they haven't got a clue
No longer will I squander my brain power.

When that Jesus comes to visit, sit a spell upon his ass
And will chat a while and maybe spend an hour.
Oh yes, then I will believe him, but until it comes to pass
No longer will I squander my brain power.

CHORUS:
No longer will I squander or will let my brain be laundered
Or in superstition wander. No, no longer will I squander my brain power.

Original Words: James M. Black, 1893

## Almost Persuaded

Almost persuaded now to believe.
Almost persuaded. Nearly deceived.
What a fancy tale they tell. Sure make it sound so swell.
For their scam I almost fell, their tale so tall.

Almost persuaded. 'Twas a close call.
Almost persuaded. Almost did fall.
Jesus would save from sin. Almost they took me in.
Sure gave it quite a spin. I've heard it all.

Almost persuaded to trust their scam.
Almost persuaded. Oh, what a sham!
Almost I fell for it. Almost I bought their shit.
Almost became a twit. What a close call.

Original Words: P. P. Bliss, 1871

## Speed the Light

To the millions living o'er the deep, deep sea speed the light. Speed the light.
And to those in our own land who fail to see speed the light. Oh, speed the light.

There in anguish millions for enlightenment wait. Speed the light. Speed the light.
Free them from religion ere it is too late. Speed the light. Oh, speed the light.

Oh, compassion bids us bear the happy news. Speed the light. Speed the light.
That religion is just a pile of refuse. Speed the light. Oh, speed the light.

CHORUS:
Speed the light, the crucial science light to the lands deep in religions' night.
Save them from their superstition's plight. Speed the light. Oh, speed the light.

Original Words: Elisha A. Hoffman

## Blast This Shame
(Tune: Precious Name)

Take the shame of Jesus with you. I don't want it anymore.
To carry it around with me is just too much of a chore.

Take the shame of Jesus with you. Walk it right out of my door.
Take it wherever you like. Just take it with you, I implore.

Take the shame of Jesus with you. No more I want folks to think
That I trust in superstitions or that I am just a dink.

CHORUS:
Blast this shame! Oh, how sweet it will be to have it gone.
Blast this shame! No more will I believe what's simply wrong.

Original Words: Lydia Baxter, 1817

# I Know That My C-Cleaner Lives
(Tune: I Know That My Redeemer Lives)

I know that my C-Cleaner lives somewhere in my PC.
Oh, what great service that it gives when it's persnickety.

It cleans things up and makes things run as smooth as they can be.
My computer is so much more fun when the garbage is emptied.

I wish a C-Cleaner they had to use on people's brains
To get rid of religion mad and free them from its chains.

Oh, if we could just empty out the superstitions people hold,
The nonsense they so often spout, it'd be worth more than gold.

Original Words: Charles Wesley, 1742

---

*I wonder who got the shit job of scouring the planet for the 15000 species of butterfly or the 8800 species of ant they eventually took on board Noah's Ark. But at least we got that magical rainbow for all their trouble.     -- Azura Skye*

---

# Love Found a Way

Wonderful love that rescued me, taught me to sin.
Guilty and vile as I can be; just makes me grin.
When ev'ry ray of light had fled, oh glorious day!
Getting that Jesus crap out of my head; love found a way.

Once I believed in Jesus' hoax like an old stooge.
Thought I was better than other folks -- ego so huge.
Then I realized that I was wrong to my dismay.
Gave up my smugness I'd held so long. Love found a way.

Love opened wide the gates of light, helped me to know
How all that Jesus crap and fright is a bunch of crow.
Love lifted me from depths of woe to times so gay.
Once all that Jesus bull I let go, love found a way.

CHORUS:
Love found a way to redeem my soul.
Love found a way that could make me whole.
Love found a way to get rid of my shame.
Love found a way to give Jesus the blame.

Original Words: Avis B. Christiansen

## Hound Him With Many Clowns
(Tune: Crown Him With Many Crowns)

Hound him with many clowns, the lamb upon his throne.
Oh, send them clowns on in to hound and make a big loud drone.
Awake, you clowns, and sing, even if it's out of key,
And as you bow and call him king don't laugh hysterically.

Hound him with many clowns at both his hands and sides.
Oh, give him lots of smiles and frowns. Hound even if he hides.
Oh, give him not a break, but ever hound him hard,
And even if he gets a headache keep acting like a card.

Hound him with many clowns, a great big circus ring
That with great sport and jests surrounds the high and mighty king.
Oh, keep him on his toes. Don't let him get away.
Don't give him peace to blow his nose. Just make him rue the day.

Original Words: Matthew Bridges, 1851

> *Scientists do not join hands every Sunday and sing "Yes gravity is real! I know gravity is real! I will have faith! I believe in my heart that what goes up, up, up must come down, down, down. Amen!" If they did, we would think they were pretty insecure about the concept*   — Dan Barker

## Is It the Clowning Day?
(Tune: Is It the Crowning Day?)

Jesus may come today. Glad day! Glad day!
And I would see my friend who keeps me laughing no end,
If Jesus should come today.

I may see him today. Glad day! Glad day!
Dressed in his cute clown suit, performing antics so cute,
If he should show up today.

Jesus may a visit pay. Glad day! Glad day!
He'll entertain us so fine, do a few tricks and some mimes,
If he should show up to play.

CHORUS:
Glad day! Glad day! Is it the clowning day?
Some nice, funny antics I would see. Jesus, my lord, our clown shall be.
Glad day! Glad day! Is it the clowning day?

Original Words: Henry Ostrom

## Oh, For a Thousand Stunts to Spring
(Tune: O For a Thousand Tongues to Sing)

Oh, for a thousand stunts to spring on my Jesus today.
Oh, I would give anything to see the face he would display.

Oh, for a thousand stunts to spring. I'd try them every one.
With each one I would hope to bring a lot of laughs and fun.

Oh, for a thousand stunts to spring on god's old church so grand.
Oh yes, I would have such a fling. Such great fun I have planned.

Oh, for a thousand stunts to spring, whenever I get bored,
On everyone who needs a laugh, but especially the lord.

Original Words: Charles Wesley, 1739

## Rusting Jesus
(Tune: Trusting Jesus)

Simply rusting every day. Rusting through a stormy way.
So much rust it does appall. Rusting Jesus, that is all.

Brightly did his spirit shine. Now his joints just creak and whine.
So rusted, can't even crawl. Rusting Jesus, that is all.

Once his way shined bright and clear. Now it seems his path is drear.
Let the rust across him sprawl. Rusting Jesus, that is all.

CHORUS
Rusting as the moments fly. Rusting as the days go by.
Rusting out whate'er befall. Rusting Jesus, that is all.

Original Words: Edgar Page Stites, 1876

## I Am Cross, Fit to Be Tied
(Tune: At the Cross I'll Abide)

Oh, Jesus, savior, what a damn pest. He really has my ass fried.
Too many buttons he has pressed. I am cross, fit to be tied.

Oh, Jesus, savior, you think you're god and can somehow save me from sin,
But really you are so very odd I want to kick you in the shin.

Oh, Jesus, savior, now take a hike somewhere far away from me.
Just head it right on down the pike or go nest in some tall tree.

CHORUS:
I am cross, fit to be tied. Forgive me if I sound snide.
I am cross, fit to be tied, meaner than Bonnie and Clyde.
I am cross. You had better hide.

Original Words: Isaiah Baltzell

## The Church's Inundation
### (Tune: The Church's One Foundation)

The church's inundation would be a sight so fine.
To wash her from creation would end her awful whine.
The end of all the nonsense of Jesus and his love.
Let's get rid of its offense and give its lies a shove.

The church's inundation could wash her from the earth,
Would end her violations and bring us joy and mirth.
No more her superstitions and dumb nonsense to hear.
Forget her stupid missions and her beliefs so queer.

The church's inundation would be a true delight,
Would stop misinformation, would end its awful blight.
And then we all could rest and forget her teachings lame.
Then we all could feel blessed to be rid of all her shame.

Original Words: S. J. Stone, 1866

## Plunder His Things
### (Tune: Under His Wings)

Plunder his things, all the things he is hiding.
Let us get ready, go crazy and wild.
Jesus is dead; he's no longer abiding.
Let's take back what from us his church has beguiled.

Plunder his things. No more will we sorrow.
With all the plunder we'll have a grand fest.
Party today and then party tomorrow,
Glad that no more by his church we're oppressed.

Plunder his things, oh what precious enjoyment!
Then we will hide while we check the loot o'er.
No longer worry about unemployment.
No longer will Jesus keep us so poor.

CHORUS:
Plunder his things. Plunder his things. What from his stuff can we sever?
Plunder his things, his gold and his rings, and we will party forever.

Original Words: William Cushing, Samuel Beck

## Can I Go Play, Lord
### (Tune: Have Thine Own Way, Lord)

Can I go play, lord? Can I go play? I'm tired of sitting in church all day.
I get so bored as the preacher drones on. I'd rather play out on the green lawn.

Can I go play, lord? Can I go play? Enjoy the playground, if that's okay.
I'd love to get serious with your word, if only it wasn't dumb and absurd.

Can I go play, lord? Can I go play? I just don't want to get holy today.
I'd rather swim or go and play tag than to be praying. It's such a drag.

Original Words: Adelaide A. Pollard, 1906

## Crave for the Blood
(Tune: Saved by the Blood)

Crave for the blood of the crucified one.
Oh, Dracula bit me and now I've begun
To sleep in my coffin, stay out of the sun,
And crave for the blood of the crucified one.

Crave for the blood of the crucified one.
With all of the vampires and werewolves I run.
Yes, sucking the blood out of humans is fun.
I crave for the blood of the crucified one.

Crave for the blood of the crucified one.
I go for the blood like Attila the Hun.
I guzzle it down, and I drink up a ton.
I crave for the blood of the crucified one.

CHORUS:
Crave! Crave! No red hemoglobin would I ever shun.
Crave! Crave! I just crave for the blood of the crucified one.

Original Words: S. J. Henderson, 1902

## What a Wonderful Flavor
(Tune: What a Wonderful Savior)

*Take, eat; this is my body. -- Matthew 26:26*

Christ has for sin atonement made. What a wonderful flavor!
His body parts are just first grade. His flavor I savor!

We serve communion at our church. What a wonderful flavor!
No better taste where'er you search. His flavor I savor!

The grape juice is his blood so fine. What a wonderful flavor!
Tastes like it came straight from the vine. His flavor I savor!

Oh, Jesus' body, that's the bread. What a wonderful flavor!
Best tasting part is Jesus' head. His flavor I savor!

The wine and bread scrumptious they be. What a wonderful flavor!
Jesus' bod is so tasty! His flavor I savor!

CHORUS:
What a wonderful flavor is Jesus, my Jesus!
What a flavor I savor of Jesus, my lord.

Original Words: Elisha A. Hoffman, 1891

## The Yellow Stream
(Tune: The Cleansing Wave)

Oh, now I see the yellow stream. The fountain from me spouts.
Just watch it glisten and gleam as my bladder empties out.

My bladder it is to be praised, gets rid of all that crud.
I look and surely am amazed at what a great big flood.

I rise to walk feeling so light to join the world and sin
With heart renewed create some blight while Jesus' crud I spin.

CHORUS:
The yellow stream I pee, I pee. I pee, and, oh, it cleanseth me!
Gets rid of all that waste in me. It cleanseth me, yes, cleanseth me.

Original Words: Phoebe Palmer

## Pesky the Guy That Whines
(Tune: Blest Be the Tie That Binds)

Pesky the guy that whines about that Christian love,
The kind that bigotry enshrines in the name of god above.

Pesky the guy that whines about god's perfect peace,
The kind that religious wars designs and makes strife and hatred increase.

Pesky the guy that whines about god's wonderful joy,
That our reason and common sense undermines and makes us our neighbors annoy.

Original Words: John Fawcett, 1782

## To Pee Like Jesus
(Tune: To Be Like Jesus)

To pee like Jesus, to pee like Jesus! My desire -- to pee like him.
Standing right up tall, piss against the wall. My desire -- to pee like him.

To pee like Jesus, to pee like Jesus! My desire -- to pee like him.
Always to shoot straight would be just so great. My desire -- to pee like him.

To pee like Jesus, to pee like Jesus! My desire -- to pee like him.
Be such a good shot. Always hit the spot. My desire -- to pee like him.

To pee like Jesus, to pee like Jesus! My desire -- to pee like him.
Never be sorry, pissing in glory. My desire -- to pee like him.

To pee like Jesus, to pee like Jesus! My desire -- to pee like him.
Never to be loud, just standing up proud. My desire -- to pee like him.

Original Words: Traditional

## What Squirmy Gyrations
(Tune: How Firm a Foundation)

What squirmy gyrations, ye saints of the lord,
You make when you preach his preposterous word.
What else can you say to more twist up the truth?
What more can you do to be rude and uncouth?

What squirmy gyrations you make when you try
To explain all of god's contradictions and lies.
What funny contortions, what creative twists
You make in your logic to make it all fit.

What squirmy gyrations. You look like a worm
When with all your crazy contortions you squirm.
What imaginations. Entertaining it is
To watch how your brains with such madness do fizz.

Original Words: Rippon's *Selection of Hymns*, 1787

---

*If you really believe that death leads to eternal bliss then why are you wearing a seatbelt?*
*-- Doug Stanhope*

---

## They Arose
(Tune: Christ Arose!)

God made the earth and sky, god, the creator.
Everything was nice as pie, god, our great lord.

Great paradise he made, god, the creator.
Peaceful each hill and glade, god, our great lord.

Adam ate from the tree, irked the creator.
All hell broke loose, you see, from our great lord.

He heated earth's inside, god the creator,
Shot rocks in a great tide, god our great lord.

Because Adam was so corrupt god, the creator,
Allowed his work to be disrupt, god, our great lord.

CHORUS:
Up from the earth they arose -- those great big and violent volcanoes.
They arose from the depths of earth's dark domain
And they erupt now to cause great death and pain.
They arose with great blows! Oh, Christ Jesus! They arose!

Original Words: Robert Lowrey, 1874

## Glorious Things of Thee Are Spoken

Glorious things of thee are spoken, Zion, city of our god.
Like a record that is broken they constantly repeat this fraud.
On the crock of ages founded, oh, how deep their bullshit flows.
I am constantly astounded how many people you can hose.

Glorious things of thee are spoken, Jesus, called the son of god.
Like a record that is broken they repeat your story flawed.
In your churches every Sunday they preach forth your stories grand.
All your myths and lies have spun they. It has gotten out of hand.

Glorious things of thee are spoken, Heaven, the abode of god.
You don't let too many folk in, only those who get god's nod.
By god's laws that place will be run. Everyone god's line must toe.
All those who are any bit fun, they go down to hell below.

Original Words: John Newton, 1779

## To Pray to the Cross, Say "Om"
(Tune: The Way of the Cross Leads Home)

I must needs go home by the way of the om. There's no other way but this.
If I ne'er get sight of the gates of light I am sure that my pants I'll piss.

I must needs go on just believing the con, the path that the savior trod.
If I ever climb to the heights sublime I must pray with that word so odd.

I must needs go pray ere I go out to play, so I set up that cross so odd.
Then I froth and foam and repeat that om 'til my soul is at one with god.

CHORUS:
To pray to the cross say, "Om". To pray to the cross say, "Om".
It is sweet to know as I onward go, to pray to the cross say, "Om".

Original Words: Jesse Brown Pounds, 1906

## I Heard the Voice of Jesus Say

I heard the voice of Jesus say, "Come unto me and rest,"
Then realized what I had to do -- went to my psychiatrist.
I came to him just as I was, so weary and worn and sad.
He said I had the religion blues and had them really bad.

I heard the voice of Jesus say, "I am this dark world's light,"
Then knew I had to get some help. It was an awful fright.
My shrink told me that he found I'd been too much in the sun.
My head was baked. My brain was fried until it was well-done.

I heard the voice of Jesus say, "Go kill your only son."
I said to him, "Yes, sir. I will," then took off in a hell of a run,
And to an asylum I turned in so I'd be safe and sound,
And so I wouldn't in his name hurt anyone around.

Original Words: Horatius Bonar, 1846

# The Lord Hears My F-Word
(Tune: The Lord Is My Shepherd)

The lord hears my F-word. He's pissed off I know.
He hates when I swear and obscenities blow.
He frowns and he scowls and gets bent out of shape.
If I keep on it really makes him go ape.
If I keep on it really makes him go ape.

The lord hears my F-word. Doesn't like it one bit.
It gets him all pissed off. He has a big fit.
I hate to upset him, but it's how I am.
Don't wish to upset him, but just don't give a damn.
Don't wish to upset him, but just don't give a damn.

The lord hears my F-word. He hates it a lot.
He says that it will cause my insides to rot.
It's F-word for this, and it's F-word for that.
If I keep using F-words my soul he will splat!
If I keep using F-words my soul he will splat!

Original Words: James Montgomery

# Part 4

## Songs for a Few

You won't want to share these songs with your Christian friends unless they have an exceptionally good sense of humor.

## How Gory, Gory Is My Lord
(Tune: Living in The Glory)

I have found a god who kills. Yes, my loving god is gory.
That is how he gets his thrills. Oh, how gory, gory is my lord.

God created men from mud. Yes, my loving god is gory.
Killed them off in a great big flood. Oh, how gory, gory is my lord.

Folks in Sodom sure got wild. Yes, my loving god is gory.
God killed every woman, man and child. Oh, how gory, gory is my lord.

God brought Israel to Canaan, Yes, my loving god is gory.
To kill them and steal their land. Oh, how gory, gory is my lord.

Uzzah saved god's ark that rocked. Yes, my loving god is gory.
God killed him right on the spot. Oh, how gory, gory is my lord.

David did what god didn't like. Yes, my loving god is gory.
Seventy thousand god did smite. Oh, how gory, gory is my lord.

David screwed Uriah's bride. Yes, my loving god is gory.
So the innocent baby died. Oh, how gory, gory is my lord.

Children laughed at Elisha's hair. Yes, my loving god is gory.
God mauled them with ugly bears. Oh, how gory, gory is my lord.

CHORUS:
Yes, my loving god is gory, as it tells us in his word.
Tick him off and you'll be sorry. Oh, how gory, gory is my lord.

Original Words: Albert B. Simpson

## Now Spank We All Our God
(Tune: Now Thank We All Our God)

Now spank we all our god with heart and hands and voices.
Spank him for what he's done, for all his evil choices,
Who from our mothers' arms has torn our kids away
And filled their heads with shit to make their brains decay.

Oh, may the evil god through all our life be near us,
So we can spank his butt, for that will surely cheer us,
To put him in his place and keep him most perplexed,
So he will never know just what we will do next.

Now many spanks to god the father now be given,
So that he will behave when he goes back to heaven.
The one infernal god, whom heaven and earth abhor,
We will keep him in line now and forevermore.

Original Words: Martin Rinckart, 1636; Translated: Catherine Winkworth

## He Is Saber-Toothed and Slithery
(Tune: He Is Able to Deliver Thee)

'Tis the grandest theme thru the ages rung.
'Tis the grandest theme for a mortal tongue.
'Tis the grandest theme that the world e'er sung:
"Our god is saber-toothed and slithery."

'Tis the grandest theme in the earth or main.
'Tis the grandest theme for a mortal strain.
'Tis the grandest theme. Tell the world again:
"Our god is saber-toothed and slithery."

'Tis the grandest theme. Let the tidings roll.
'Tis the grandest theme: "Our god is a troll."
'Tis the grandest theme: He'll bite in you a hole.
Our god is saber-toothed and slithery.

CHORUS:
He is saber-toothed and slithery.
He is saber-toothed and slithery.
Slither up your chest or bite you in the breast.
Our god is saber-toothed and slithery.

Original Words: W. A. Ogden, 1887

## The Dumb Flirter Has Come
(Tune: The Comforter Has Come)

Oh, spread the tidings round wherever man is found.
The dumb flirter has come, as dumb as an old hound.
Oh when he tries to flirt he just acts like a clown.
The dumb flirter has come.

The long, long days are past. The night is here at last.
So now we will go out and try to have a blast.
That dumb flirter's so dumb, though, he can't make a pass.
The dumb flirter has come.

Lo, the poor thing of flings, with flirting in his wings,
To every horny soul he stupid flirting brings.
Yet, to his sorry lines and dumb methods he clings.
The dumb flirter has come.

CHORUS:
The dumb flirter has come. The dumb flirter has come.
The holy ghost from heaven, Casper's little cousin.
Dumb as an old hound. He just acts like a clown.
The dumb flirter has come.

Original Words: Joe Blow, 1888

## God Leads His Queer Children All Wrong
(Tune: God Leads His Dear Children Along)

With shady ideas he pitches so sweet
God leads his queer children all wrong.
He tramples them daily right under his feet.
God leads his queer children all wrong.

Sometimes on the mount he says things not so bright.
God leads his queer children all wrong.
Sometimes in the valley their asses he'll bite.
God leads his queer children all wrong.

Though sorrows befall us and Satan oppose
God leads his queer children all wrong.
We'll flick him our boogers and spit on his nose.
God leads his queer children all wrong.

Oh, into the mire and onto the clay,
God leads his queer children all wrong.
Even so go god's queer folks when him they obey.
God leads his queer children all wrong.

CHORUS:
Some thru the waters, some thru the flood,
Some thru the fire. He's just such a dud!
Through god's fiascos we'll just sing our song,
When our god leads his queer children all wrong.

Original Words: G. A. Young

## A Mighty Tortoise Is Our God
(Tune: A Mighty Fortress Is Our God)

A mighty tortoise is our god. A big strong shell he carries.
A nice safe place where he can go to hide when it gets scary.
For when our ancient foe doth seek to work us woe,
Whose craft and pow'r are great and armed with cruel hate,
God gets afraid so easily.

We must in our own strength confide though our striving be losing,
For he who should be on our side seems always to be snoozing.
Dost ask who that may be? Christ Jesus, it is he,
Lord Slobosloth his name, from age to age the same,
A loser who does nothing.

And though this world with devils filled should threaten to undo us,
We will not fear such chumps unskilled when god's already screwed us.
The prince of darkness grim, we tremble not for him.
His rage we can endure, for he is full of spoor,
Just like our god the tortoise.

Original Words: Martin Luther, 1529 (Frederick H. Ledge, translator, 1852)

## I Am a Deadbeat Dad
(Tune: Lead On, O King Eternal)

I am a deadbeat dad! Oh, I'm just a deadbeat dad!
My kids they never see me. They think that I'm a cad.
Oh, while they suffer daily I just hang out above.
I am a deadbeat dad. I am the great god of love.

I am a deadbeat dad! Oh, I'm just a deadbeat dad!
Five senses I gave my kids. That's all they ever had.
And never do I let them through those senses me know.
I am a deadbeat dad. Never I my face will show.

I am a deadbeat dad! Oh, I'm just a deadbeat dad!
My children I would visit, but I just get so mad.
So I just leave them to whatever may be their fate.
I am a deadbeat dad. I am their god who's so great.

Original Words: Ernest W. Shurtleff, 1887

## Please Spare Me, Breath of God
(Tune: Breathe on Me, Breath of God)

Please spare me, breath of god. Don't breathe on me your spew.
Your old breath, it just smells so odd, smells like a sweaty shoe.

Please spare me, breath of god. Listerine makes you pure.
Right now you smell like rotting cod. Your stench I can't endure

Please spare me, breath of god, so I don't pass out and die.
For it is like your smelly bod, just like an old pig sty.

Original Words: Edwin Hatch, 1878

## Near to the Fart of God
(Tune: Near to the Heart of God)

There is a place of funny smells near to the fart of god,
A place where stench most fetid swells near to the fart of god.

There is a place of bad odors near to the fart of god,
A place that every nose abhors near to the fart of god.

There is a place of full release near to the fart of god,
A place not safe for man nor beast near to the fart of god.

CHORUS:
Oh, Jesus, blessed redeemer, what is that smell so odd?
Is it because we got too near to the fart of god?

Original Words: Cleland Boyd McAfee, 1903

## When Mourning Fills the Skies
(Tune: When Morning Gilds the Skies)

When mourning fills the skies you know that god is nigh. He is so goddam crazed.
Alike at work and prayer he's so awful, I swear. He is so goddam crazed.

Does sadness fill my mind? You bet your old behind! He is so goddam crazed.
What fades my earthly bliss? It's all his rot and piss. He is so goddam crazed.

When reason he denies my silent spirit sighs, "He is so goddam crazed."
When god does us molest I am greatly distressed. He is so goddam crazed.

In night as well as day his horrors he'll display. He is so goddam crazed.
He is something to fear. With hatred he does sneer. He is so goddam crazed.

Now this question is mine: Why he treats us like swine? He is so goddam crazed.
And so this is my song, that trusting him is wrong. He is so goddam crazed.

Original Words: Edward Caswall, 1854

## Lead On, Oh King Infernal
(Tune: Lead On, O King Eternal)

Lead on, oh king infernal; the day of march has come.
We follow where you lead, just because we are so dumb.
Through days of preparation thy lies have made us strong.
So we will follow you and sing loud our foolish song.

Lead on, oh king infernal; hell of a king you are.
You'll lead us all through hell if we follow you that far.
Oh, those who join your army are not the brightest kind.
They follow superstition with faith that is so blind.

Lead on, oh king infernal; we follow, what the hell!
No matter how you beat us, no matter how you smell.
We follow you in lock step no matter what you say.
Just put our brains in neutral, your foolishness obey.

Original Words: Ernest W. Shurtleff, 1887

## Son of a Troll
(Tune: Sun of My Soul)

Son of a troll, thou savior queer, it's such a fright when thou be near.
Oh, may some earth-born clown arise and poke thee square between the eyes.

Be far from me from morn 'til eve, so I don't have to put up with your peeves.
Be far from me when night is nigh, for without thee I feel so high.

When the soft dews of kindly sleep my weary eyelids gently steep,
Be my last thought -- how sweet to rest without that troll. He's such a pest.

Original Words: John Keble, 1820

## Jesus, You Are Such a Troll
(Tune: Jesus Lover of My Soul)

Jesus, you are such a troll. Carry in your bosom flies.
With great care your boogers roll. Up your nose you stuff French fries.
Hide now, oh my savior, hide in your secret troll abode.
Burrow safely down inside 'til I do my shotgun load.

Jesus, you are such a troll, with your dark and beady eyes.
With great pleasure out you dole all the mischief you devise.
Blackmail them with threats of hell. Pay ten percent of all they earn.
Hide the truth 'neath lies you tell. Confuse them with nonsense you churn.

Jesus, you are such a troll, under bridges hiding out.
Won't you go back to your hole? Go smear slime balls on your snout.
Hide now, oh, my troll, go hide. No more trouble cause us now.
Spare us all your scheme so snide. Tell it to some dumb old cow.

Original Words: Charles Wesley, 1740

> *I have examined all the known superstitions of the world, and I do not find in our particular superstition of Christianity one redeeming feature. They are all alike founded on fables and mythology.*
>
> *-- Thomas Jefferson*

## Helter-Skelter in a Slimy Moor
(Tune: A Shelter in the Time of Storm)

The lord's a crock; from him we hide. Helter-skelter in a slimy moor.
How many from his teeth have died? Helter-skelter in a slimy moor.

He hides out in a muddy swamp. Helter-skelter in a slimy moor.
Waiting for prey on whom to chomp. Helter-skelter in a slimy moor.

Terror by day, horror by night. Helter-skelter in a slimy moor.
Always causing alarm and fright. Helter-skelter in a slimy moor.

The raging storms may round us beat. Helter-skelter in a slimy moor.
From him there is no safe retreat. Helter-skelter in a slimy moor.

Alligators are perverse. Helter-skelter in a slimy moor.
But crocs like him are even worse. Helter-skelter in a slimy moor.

CHORUS:
Oh, Jesus is a crock in a miry land, a miry land, a miry land.
Oh, Jesus is a crock in a miry land. Helter-skelter in a slimy moor.

Original Words: Vernon J. Charlesworth, c. 1880

## Savior, Like a Shepherd Lead Us

Savior, like a shepherd lead us, while we cuss and bitch and swear,
To the slaughterhouse to bleed us, then the lamb chops to prepare.
Bloody Jesus, bloody Jesus, oh, how bloodthirsty you are.
Bloody Jesus, bloody Jesus, you're the most cruel by far.

Savior, like a shepherd lead us. To you we're nothing but livestock.
Hateful is the way you treat us, enough one's conscience to shock.
Bloody Jesus, bloody Jesus, oh, now hear us when we pray.
Bloody Jesus, bloody Jesus, would you please just go away.

Savior, like a shepherd lead us in your lies and myths so grand.
All the bullshit that you feed us 'til in the slaughterhouse we land.
Bloody Jesus, bloody Jesus, we will early turn to thee.
Bloody Jesus, bloody Jesus, then fast from you we will flee.

Original Words: Dorothy A. Thrupp, 1836

## Shun That Unsightly Thing
(Tune: Come, Thou Almighty King)

Shun that unsightly thing. Watch out that it does not sting.
Jesus the lord. See how he sorry is.
See how he gory is. What a sad story 'tis -- sadly abhorred.

Shun that unsightly thing. Be careful it does not spring
Onto your head, digging and pawing,
Scratching and clawing, grinding and gnawing until you are dead.

Shun that unsightly thing. And all the crap it does sling.
And does confuse us who are fool enough
To catch his gooey stuff, who don't eschew the guff religion spews.

Original Words: Anonymous

## All Stale and Sour Is Jesus' Name
(Tune: All Hail the Power of Jesus' Name)

All stale and sour is Jesus' name. It went bad long ago.
Let's clean it up, no matter who's to blame, and in the trash it throw.
Let's clean it up, no matter who's to blame, and in the trash it throw.

All stale and sour is Jesus' name. It has begun to smell.
Oh, let us get rid of this shame, and let's its stench expel.
Oh, let us get rid of this shame, and let's its stench expel.

All stale and sour is Jesus' name. It has begun to rot.
For all his claims -- they are so lame. His reputation's gone to pot.
For all his claims -- they are so lame. His reputation's gone to pot.

Original Words: Edward Perronet, 1780

## Where Jesus Is 'Tis Quite a Scare
(Tune: Where Jesus Is 'Tis Heaven There)

Since Christ was from the zoo set free this old world sure has been scary.
And when you hear of dread and woe, it's because he is free below.

Once heaven seemed a far off place -- oh, somewhere far off out in space,
But Jesus found his way to earth and now stocks us for all he's worth.

What matters where on earth we dwell? On mountaintop or in the dell,
Stand on the roof, hide in the well, where Jesus is, 'tis surely hell.

CHORUS:
Oh my god, it is scary now, since that Jesus got loose somehow.
On land or sea, what matters where? Where Jesus is, 'tis quite a scare.

Original Words: Charles F. Butler

## Big Brouhaha, What Behavior!
(Tune: Hallelujah, What a Savior)

"Man of trouble," what a name for the son of god who came
A big turmoil to enflame. Big brouhaha. What behavior!

Bearing shame and scoffing rude because of his antics lewd.
How much trouble has he stewed? Big brouhaha. What behavior!

Guilty, vile and mean was he. Innocent victims are we.
When will end his evil spree? Big brouhaha. What behavior!

Original Words: P. P. Bliss, 1875

## Make Slime Roly-Polies
(Tune: Take Time To Be Holy)

Make slime, roly-polies, like Jesus our lord.
More slime you will make the more you feed on his word.
You'll make lots of nice slime though you may be weak,
If you just remember his slime to go seek.

Make slime, roly-polies. The world rushes on,
But you take the time to make slime and to spawn.
By looking to Jesus, like him thou shalt be,
Exuding your slime and fool notions with glee.

Make slime, roly-polies. Be calm in thy souls.
Be easy and gentle in each of your rolls.
Lay down lots of nice slime. Whenever you do
Just remember Jesus is slimy like you.

Original Words: William D. Longstaff, c. 1882

## Hiding From Thee
(Tune: Hiding in Thee)

In space there's a rock way out beyond the sky.
To get away from Jesus' crap there would I fly.
How far away is it I have to go flee?
Thou pest, crock of ages, I'm hiding from thee.

In the calm of the noontide, in sorrow's lone hour,
My spaceship I make ready. I beef up its power
So that when I need to I can move rapidly.
Thou pest, crock of ages, I'm hiding from thee.

How oft in the conflict, when pressed by the foe,
I will jump in my spaceship. Far off I will go
To get away from Jesus, that troublesome troll,
That pest, crock of ages. Then I'll rock and roll.

CHORUS:
Hiding from thee. Hiding from thee.
Thou pest, crock of ages, I'm hiding from thee.

Original Words: W. O. Cushing, 1876

## Barest Lord Jesus
(Tune: Fairest Lord Jesus)

Barest Lord Jesus, getting down to nature, getting a tan underneath the sun,
Letting it all hang out, even on the glacier. In the buff is lots of fun.

Barest Lord Jesus, barer than the woodlands, or even grasslands or deserts dry,
Taking off all his clothes so he gets a good tan. He's such a sexy, well-toned guy.

Barest Lord Jesus, lounging in the sunshine, with every inch exposed to the sun.
Vitamin D he'll get and have a tan so fine on his chest and back and buns.

Original Words: Unknown source

## Must Jesus Swear and Cuss Alone
(Tune: Must Jesus Bear the Cross Alone)

Must Jesus swear and cuss alone and all the world go free?
No, there's a cuss for everyone, and he can swear with me.

How happy are the saints above, as well as those down here,
When they can cuss and swear in love and blaspheme in your ear.

This burden to curse I will bear 'til death shall set me free
To help Jesus to cuss and swear. Yes, he can cuss with me.

Original Words: Thomas Shepherd, 1693

## Jesus Phony
(Tune: Jesus Only)

Jesus phony is our message. Jesus, oh, how queer is he.
We will laugh at Jesus ever. He our greatest joke will be.

Jesus, phony as a savior, couldn't save a poor lost blue jay
But that won't cause us to waver from trying our balderdash to lay.

Jesus, phony as a healer, like a witch-doctor with bones in his hair.
He is such a shady dealer, full of bat shit and lots of hot air.

CHORUS:
Jesus phony, not so clever, Jesus what a joke we sing.
The biggest cock and bull story ever. What a silly ridiculous thing.

Original Words: Albert Benjamin Simpson

## I Saw the Cross of Jesus

I saw the cross of Jesus. It makes great firewood.
I saw the cross of Jesus. It builds a fire good.
I saw the cross of Jesus after washing off his blood,
But most of all I saw it to get rid of all his crud.

I saw the cross of Jesus. A good sawyer I am.
And then I'll build a fire to roast up my fresh lamb.
No righteousness nor merit, no beauty can I plead,
But it will sure be tasty when upon it I do feed.

I saw the cross of Jesus, even with my weary heart.
I saw the cross of Jesus 'til wholly sawn apart.
And then in strains of glory with all my human power
I'll build a nice big fire and that lamb I will devour.

Original Words: Frederick Whitfield

## Stand Up for Jesus

Stand up, stand up for Jesus. He can't stand on his own.
Oh, when he tries to get up he'll stumble, creak and moan.
He's such a poor old fellow. After two thousand years
Just trying to stand up will bring him right to tears.

Stand up, stand up for Jesus. The trumpet call obey.
He needs you to stand for him, for his bones have decayed.
The poor old guy just ain't got it in him anymore.
He's just too old and feeble. His bones are way too sore.

Stand up, stand up for Jesus. Oh, stand up for our god.
He'd stand up for himself, but he's got a real old bod.
Take pity on his weakness. He's just not doing well,
So do his standing for him, so he can rest a spell.

Original Words: George Duffield, 1858

# One Day!

One day when heaven was filled with rapscallions,
One day when sin was so certain to please,
Jesus claimed to have been born of a virgin.
Won't someone teach him the birds and the bees?

One day he climbed to the top of a mountain.
One day he climbed to the top of a tree.
Suffering anguish, despised and rejected,
Sat on a limb, and he chewed on his knee.

One day they left him alone in the garden.
One day they left him to run around free.
Angels came down, and they helped him dig turnips.
What a good old turnip digger was he.

CHORUS:
Living, he preached shit. Dying, the dust he bit.
Buried, his myth just should have died away.
Rising up from his myth came a great scam forthwith.
One day we'll wake up. Oh, glorious day!

Original Words: J. Wilbur Chapman, 1910

> *Give a man a fish and he will eat for a day; teach a man to fish and he will eat for a lifetime; give a man religion and he will die praying for a fish.*
> *-- Benjamin Disraeli*

# Jesus Is Like a Squirrel to Me
(Tune: Jesus Is All the World to Me)

Jesus is like a squirrel to me, so funny, cute and small.
He entertains me day to day. His antics do me enthrall.
When I am sad I watch him go. All of his frolics cheer me so.
When I am sad he's just a cad. He's so cute!

Jesus is like a squirrel to me, as nutso as can be
If he does frolic on the lawn or go climb up a tree.
Doesn't seem to know what to do. Just runs around with a loose screw.
What will he do? Such a loose screw. He's a fruit.

Jesus is like a squirrel to me. Lots of nuts he does store.
He gathers them into his church, bamboozles them o'er and o'er.
He gathers them in sun and rain, disconnects the use of their brains.
Nonsense he rains upon their brains. He's a brute.

Original Words: Will L. Thompson, 1904

## Oh, How I Love Jesus

There is a name I love to hear. I love to sing its worth.
It sounds like music in my ear, since I'm with bad hearing cursed.

It tells me of a savior's love, who died to set me free,
And now way up my rear does shove his stupid nonsense with glee.

It tells me of a father's smile while beating on his child,
And how that every once in a while he gets right down and wild.

It tells of one whose loving heart can feel my deepest woe,
And how in my face he loves to fart, then throw me out in the snow.

There is a name I love to hear. It gives me such a big laugh
To think about Jesus, oh so queer, and his followers so daft.

CHORUS:
Oh, how I love Jesus. Give him lots of big squeezes.
Oh, how I love Jesus, because I'm as dumb as a flea.

Original Words: Frederick Whitfield

> *Which is it, is man one of God's blunders or is God one of man's?* -- Friedrich Nietzsche

## Oh, How I Love Jesus

There is a name I love to hear. I love to use it to curse.
Just make me angry; I'll fill your ear with the sweetest name on earth.

His name's so very dear to me, it makes me break out in sweat.
It gets me so hot and bothered, I do things I'll surely regret.

Oh, Jesus' name is so dear to me, I love it so much I swear.
When I do hear it it makes me pee right down in my underwear.

Oh, Jesus is such a good boy. His name is close to my heart.
He fills me with such love and joy it makes me want to fart.

CHORUS:
Oh, how I love Jesus -- full of gooey, gooshy puss.
Oh, how I love Jesus, because I'm as dumb as a flea.

Original Words: Frederick Whitfield

> *I don't know if God exists, but it would be better for his reputation if he didn't.* -- Jules Renard

## Wonderful, Nitwitted Friend
(Tune: Wonderful, Unfailing Friend)

There never was a screwier friend than Jesus.
He hears me when my heart for good jokes whines (for good jokes whines).
And no one makes me laugh as much as Jesus,
For he alone comes through with the best lines.

There never was a screwier friend than Jesus.
The strangest things he'll always with me share (ways with me share).
When I ask him to speak plainly my Jesus
Looks at me with a blank and empty stare.

There never was a screwier friend than Jesus.
He says he wants to take my sins away (my sins away).
Oh, what a silly goofball is my Jesus.
Does not realize I love to in sin play.

CHORUS:
Wonderful, nitwitted friend is Jesus. What funny things he always has to say.
Wonderful, hair-brained friend is Jesus. He keeps me laughing all the way.

Original Words: Albert Simpson Reitz

> *The easy confidence with which I know another man's religion is folly teaches me to suspect that my own is also.*    -- Mark Twain

## Still Sweeter Every Day

To Jesus every day I find my mouth is closer drawn.
He's tastier than steamed lobster, even garnished with prawns.
Loaded with sugar he's so sweet, sweeter even than s'mores.
Each day he tastes still sweeter than he did the day before.

He's sweeter than a chocolate cake, oh, much sweeter by far.
He's sweeter than a Hershey's kiss or any candy bar.
He's sweeter still than any treat from your convenience store.
Each day he tastes still sweeter than he did the day before.

My heart is sometimes heavy, but to chew him brings relief.
Just sucking down that sugary treat, it lightens up my grief.
His sweet and gooey nougat tastes good right down to the core.
Each day he tastes still sweeter than he did the day before.

CHORUS:
The half cannot be fancied without wanting some more.
Oh, there he'll taste still sweeter than he ever did before.

Original Words: William C. Martin

# I Have Decided to Swallow Jesus
## (Tune: I Have Decided to Follow Jesus)

I have decided to swallow Jesus.
I have decided to swallow Jesus.
I have decided to swallow Jesus.
No turning back. No turning back.

Though none chew for me, I still will swallow.
Though none chew for me, I still will swallow.
Though none chew for me, I still will swallow.
No turning back. No turning back.

My fork I'll carry 'til I eat Jesus.
My fork I'll carry 'til I eat Jesus.
My fork I'll carry 'til I eat Jesus.
No turning back. No turning back.

The bones behind me. The meat inside me.
The bones behind me. The meat inside me.
The bones behind me. The meat inside me.
No turning back. No turning back.

Original Words: Anonymous

# I Love to Tell the Story

I love to tell the story of unseen things above,
Because fooling and gulling is something that I love.
I love to tell the story, though I know it's not true.
'Cause telling big tall tales is just something that I do.

I love to tell the story. How wonderful it seems.
More crazy it is than your most convoluted dreams.
I love to tell the story. It does so much for me
To hoodwink and bamboozle. It just fills me with glee.

I love to tell the story. 'Tis pleasant to repeat.
To fill your mind with hogwash just is to me so sweet.
I love to tell the story. When those who've never heard
Fall for the con I give them it's such fun. Oh, my word!

I love to tell the story, for those who know it best
Seem hungering and thirsting this nonsense to express.
I love to tell the story. When I sing you my song
I'll laugh with great abandon as you figure out what's wrong.

CHORUS:
I love to tell the story. 'Twill be my theme in glory
To tell you, oh, how sorry is Jesus and his love.

Original Words: Kate Hankey (1866); William G. Fischer (1869) (refrain)

## A New Game So Sorry
(Tune: A New Name in Glory)

I was once a sinner, but I came flimflam to receive from my god.
This was freely given, and I found I could be part of his fraud (of his fraud)!

I was humbly kneeling at the cross, fearing naught but god's angry frown,
When my eyes were opened, and I saw he was nothing but a clown (but a clown)!

In the book 'tis written, "Saved by grace." Oh, the joy that came to my soul.
Now I am forgiven, and I know lots of hogwash I can dole (I can dole).

CHORUS:
There's a new game bound to make you sorry, and it's mine. Oh yes, it's mine.
So just listen as I tell a tall story like a good little gnome.
For there's a new game bound to make you sorry, and it's mine. Oh yes, it's mine.
With the spew I'm givin' to madness you'll be driven 'til at the mouth you foam.

Original Words: C. Austin Miles

## Only Trust Him

Come, every soul who feels oppressed. From Jesus don't recoil.
He has a remedy that's best. He'll sell you his snake oil.

For Jesus shed his precious blood to fill our bottles full,
So we now can the market flood if you'll just buy our bull.

Come, then, and buy our special brand that from Jesus did flow,
And let's create a big demand, so we'll make lots of dough.

CHORUS:
Only trust him, snake oil salesman. Only trust him now.
Buy his snake oil. Don't let it spoil. Buy his snake oil now.

Original Words: J. H. Stockton, 1874

## Deeper and Deeper

Under the myths of Jesus deeper and deeper I'm snowed,
Seeking to know the reason why such bull crap has flowed,
Why he should stoop to such lies, turning my mind to clay.
Pesky old troll, on he does droll 'til my mind's eaten away.

Under the spell of Jesus, deeper and deeper I'm snowed,
Praying for grace to follow him down the yellow brick road.
Bowing in full surrender, so that he won't me beat,
Bidding him take a jump in the lake with big rocks tied to his feet.

Into the snare of Jesus deeper and deeper I'm snowed,
Following through the garden, stomping him like a toad.
It gives me so much sorrow, leaves me with broken heart.
Oh, savior, help! Don't feed me kelp or spank me to make my ass smart.

Original Words: Oswald J. Smith

## I Schemed. How I Love to Proclaim It!
(Tune: Redeemed, How I Love to Proclaim It)

I schemed. How I love to proclaim it! I schemed on the blood of the lamb.
I schemed without a shred of mercy. Oh, what a great schemer I am.

I schemed. I'm so happy in Jesus no language my rapture can tell.
The joy of my scheming for Jesus with me doth continually dwell.

I schemed for my blessed redeemer. I schemed for him all the day long.
I schemed, for I cannot be silent. His scheme is the theme of my song.

CHORUS:
I schemed! I schemed! I schemed on the blood of the lamb.
I schemed! I schemed! And, oh, how I run a great scam!

Original Words: Fanny Crosby, 1882

## I'll Troll Where You Want Me to Troll
(Tune: I'll Go Where You Want Me to Go)

It may not be on the mountain's height or over the stormy sea.
It may not be at the battle's front my lord will have need of me.
But if by a still, small voice he calls to paths I do not know
I'll answer, dear lord, with my hand in thine, "I'll troll where you want me to troll."

Perhaps today there are crafty words which Jesus would have me speak.
There may be now, in the paths of sin, some wand'rer whom out I can freak.
Oh savior, if thou wilt be my guide, tho' dark and rugged the way,
My voice shall echo the message sly, "I'll prey on who you want me to prey."

There's surely somewhere a lowly place in earth's harvest fields so wide
Where I may labor thru' life's short day for Jesus, the one so snide.
So trusting my all to thy wily care, and knowing thy hoax won't cease,
I'll do thy will with a fart and a sneer. I'll fleece who you want me to fleece.

CHORUS:
I'll troll where you want me to troll, dear lord, o'er mountain or plain or seas.
I'll prey on who you want me to prey, dear lord. I'll fleece who you want me to fleece.

Original Words: Mary Brown

## What a Fib Uproarious
(Tune: Like a River Glorious)

What a fib uproarious -- there's a god of peace.
Fable so preposterous just seems to increase.
Preposterous, it makes me wonder every day.
Preposterous, it keeps me laughing all the way.

What a fib uproarious -- we are in god's hands.
Never such a story so crazy and grand.
Such a load of hogwash, makes me want to cry
To hear folks spout nonsense, reality deny.

What a fib uproarious. I just piss my pants
Every time I hear their stories or their rants.
What a cockamamie story do they tell --
God does surely love us -- sends us all to hell.

CHORUS:
Fairy god Jehovah, such a bully pest
If he just existed, so just give it a rest.

Original Words: Frances Ridley Havergal

## Only Trust Him

Come, every soul, and be depressed by trusting in the lord. For
he is such a lousy pest. He'll keep you ever bored.

For Jesus, they say, shed his blood, put on a great big show,
So you can believe in this crud and eat a lot of crow.

Come, then, and join this witless band, and Jesus' line we'll toe,
While slaving under his big hand and he enjoys the show.

CHORUS:
Only trust him. Only trust him. Only trust him now.
He'll enslave you. He'll enslave you. He'll enslave you now.

Original Words: J. H. Stockton, 1874

## What a Hoax!
(Tune: Christ Arose!)

Low in the grave he lay, Jesus, the savior,
Starting to rot away, Jesus, the lord.

Vainly they watch his bed, Jesus, the savior.
Like a doornail he's dead -- Jesus, the lord.

"Keep you alive," they pray. "Jesus, our savior.
Somehow we'll find a way, Jesus, our lord."

CHORUS:
Then what a great hoax arose. Even in this day people it snows.
They say he arose up from the dark domain,
So the limits of insanity they strain.
Listen folks! It's no joke! Oh, Christ Jesus! What a hoax!

Original Words: Robert Lowrey, 1874

## At the Cross

Alas, and did my brain cells bleed and did my intellect die
When I accepted Christian creed and did their hogwash buy?

Was it for crimes that I had done they took my sense from me?
But that's alright. I'll just have fun in my stupidity.

Who needs to think or reason clear when myths you can believe.
Don't worry that they are so queer. Just trust the tales they weave.

CHORUS:
At the cross, at the cross where my mind they did blight,
And the thinking of my brain took away.
It was there by faith I became not so bright,
And now I am happy all the day!

Original Words: Issac Watts, 1707

## Jesus Giveth Us the Fib Story
### (Tune: Jesus Giveth Us the Victory)

There's a story spreading throughout many places.
With his phony fables they will lead you on,
Telling you their hogwash with smiles upon their faces.
Will you fall for all their gibberish and con?

Faith is what they say you need to get to heaven.
On our sweet old Jesus you should your faith lay.
Just empty your brain and blind faith rest your head in.
Then in blissful ignorance you'll be so gay.

Let us take the fib story to every kingdom
Tell them that they need to stop their lives of sin.
Then they can join with us in our song and sing dumb,
Helping us spread nonsense with a silly grin.

CHORUS:
Jesus giveth us the fib story.
He who pulled the wool over their eyes pulls the wool again over you and I.
He'll sure screw ya! Jesus gives the fib story.

Original Words: Albert Benjamin Simpson

# Tell Me a Big, Tall Story
(Tune: Tell Me the Old, Old Story)

Tell me a big, tall story of unseen things above,
Of Jesus and his glory, of Jesus and his love.
Tell me the story simply, as to a little child,
For I have to think like one if I will be so beguiled.

Tell me the story clearly. I cannot help but grin,
For it's so hard to swallow such an incredible spin.
Tell me the story often. It's such a stupendous lie.
It's such a bunch of malarkey I laugh until I cry.

Tell me the story slowly. I want to hear every word.
I get such a kick out of it, because it is so absurd.
I double over laughing. The tears come to my eyes.
It's better than the Sunday comics, it's such a big crock of lies.

CHORUS:
Tell me a big, tall story. Tell me a great big story.
Tell me a whopper of a story, of Jesus and his love.

Original Words: Kate Hankey

> *God ... The omnipotent, omniscient, omnipresent, all-wise, infinite mind who—for strictly personal reasons—makes a point of seeming to be an impotent, know-nothing, nowhere, bumbling oaf.*
> *-- Rev. Donald Morgan*

# Nothing but the Crud
(Tune: Nothing but the Blood)

What could be a greater sin? Nothing but the crud of Jesus.
What lie has a bigger spin? Nothing but the crud of Jesus.

For my garden this I see. Nothing but the crud of Jesus.
Such great shit I do decree. Nothing but the crud of Jesus.

This is all my hope and peace. Nothing but the crud of Jesus.
That someday his crud will cease. Nothing but the crud of Jesus.

CHORUS:
Oh, how vile is the flow that my mind tries to snow.
What makes you swallow crow? Nothing but the crud of Jesus.

Original Words: Robert Lowry, 1876

## Come Jive Us Again
(Tune: Revive Us Again)

You're crazy, oh god. You claim that you are love,
Then shit loads of jive up our asses you shove.

We're crazy, oh god, to believe in your crap,
To fall into your snare and let it our minds trap.

They're crazy, oh god, those who buy our sly line.
Watching them getting duped is a joy oh so fine.

It's crazy, you see, to believe in such bull.
Oh, and what a great trip such a mad trick to pull.

It's crazy, oh god. Those who fall for our farce.
Those with heads in the sand and intelligence so sparse.

CHORUS:
Hallelujah! What a story! Howdy do ya? Amen!
Has it screwed ya? Oh, good glory! Come, jive us again.

Original Words: W. P. MacKay, 1863, 1867

> *Is God willing to prevent evil, but not able? Then he is not omnipotent.*
> *Is he able, but not willing? Then he is malevolent.*
> *Is he both able and willing? Then whence cometh evil?*
> *Is he neither able nor willing? Then why call him God?*
> -- Epicurus

## Joy Unspeakable

I have found his myth is all so neat, just as good as the best weed.
And in my mouth I put my feet and spout his crazy creed.

I have found the pleasure I once craved. It is joy and peace within.
And I feel so wondrously depraved as his slick, smooth tales I spin.

I have found the joy no tongue can tell. How its waves of glory roll!
While his malarkey I now do sell to any buying soul.

CHORUS:
It is joy unspeakable and full of glory, full of glory, full of glory.
It is joy unspeakable and full of glory. Oh, the half has never yet been told!

Original Words: Barney Elliot Warren, 1900

## A Lot of Crock
(Tune: The Solid Rock)

My hope is built on nothingness. That's Jesus' blood and righteousness.
I wholly lean on Jesus' name, though it is so damn weak and lame.

When darkness veils his lovely face I just rely on my blind faith
Even if in the stormy gale his promises just seem to fail.

His oath, his covenant, his blood, his whole religion is a dud.
Why do I keep on in this way? Because my brain cells have decayed.

CHORUS:
On Christ, a bunch of crock, I stand.
My head is buried in the sand. My head is buried deep in the sand.

Original Words: Edward Mote, 1834

## Crock of Ages
(Tune: Rock of Ages)

Crock of ages, fantasy, let me fool myself with thee.
For I really have been snowed by your falsehoods which have flowed.
Will my naiveté be cured, or is my brain forever skewered?

Crock of ages, lunacy, what a crock of bull is thee.
Some man dying on a cross somehow makes my sins be lost.
I buy this, because my mind resides down in my behind.

Crock of ages, naively I have put my faith in thee.
No more will I use my brain. It's just too much of a strain.
Just accept with faith so blind and so put to sleep my mind.

Original Words: Augustus Toplady, 1776

## Come and Dine

Jesus has a table spread where the saints of god are fed.
He invites his chosen people, "Come and dine."
With his bullshit he does feed, stuffs us with his foolish creed.
What a gag to sup with Jesus all the time.

The disciples came to land, thus obeying Christ's command,
For the master called unto them, "Come and dine."
There they found their hearts' desire, bread and fish upon the fire,
But to eat they had to listen to his whine.

Soon the lamb will take his bride to be ever at his side.
All the host of heaven will assembled be.
Oh, 'twill be a glorious sight when that lamb gets all uptight,
And upon all of their heads he does then pee.

**CHORUS:**
"Come and dine," the master calleth, "Come and dine."
You may eat up Jesus' bullshit all the time.
He who fed the multitude, gave them hogwash, oh so fine
To the naïve calleth now, "Come and dine."

Original Words: C. B. Widmeyer, 1907

# Since the Bullshit of His Love They Spin
### (Tune: Since the Fullness of His Love Came In)

Once my way was bright and cheery, for my heart was full of sin,
But the sky is dark and dreary since the bullshit of his love they spin.

It's disgrace for all the lowly and each other trusting soul,
To put their beliefs wholly under religion's dreadful control.

They proclaim their silly story, tall tales with their silly grin.
It's a fiasco so sorry since the bullshit of his love they spin.

**CHORUS:**
I can never tell how much I love him. I can never tell his love for me.
For they should just drown such liars in the deep, unfathomed sea.
'Tis a foolish tale of Christ the savior. I just laugh whenever they begin,
And I shake my head in wonder since the bullshit of his love they spin.

Original Words: E. E. Hewitt, 1916

# Cussed Insurance
### (Tune: Blessed Assurance)

Cussed insurance, at least is mine.
When you do need them your claim they decline.
Much like the Bible, claimed word of god,
Never comes through. It's just a big fraud.

Cussed insurance. Just a big scam.
Give them your money. They don't give a damn.
Much like Christ Jesus, savior they say,
Too busy golfing when you do pray.

Cussed insurance! Waste of your dough.
All that they do is screw you over so.
Just like religion, gives you the shaft --
Promises much, but then burns your ass.

**CHORUS:**
This is my story. This is my song: When I do need him he's smoking his bong.
This is my story. This is my song: Trusting in Jesus simply is wrong.

Original Words: Fanny J. Crosby

## Since Jesus Came Into My Heart

What a wonderful change in my life has been wrought
Since Jesus came into my heart.
I can feel him inside when he sits on the pot
Since Jesus came into my heart.

I have ceased from my wanderings and going astray
Since Jesus came into my heart.
I have Jesus inside and so now I am gay
Since Jesus came into my heart.

I'm as happy as a worm in a big pile of turds
Since Jesus came into my heart.
I just turn off my brain, listen to all his words
Since Jesus came into my heart.

How blissful I am in my ignorance pure
Since Jesus came into my heart.
All my brain cells have now just turned into manure
Since Jesus came into my heart.

CHORUS:
Since Jesus came into my heart
I feel it each time he does fart.
Floods of joy o'er my soul like the sea billows roll
Each time Jesus farts in my heart.

Original Words: Rufus H. McDaniel, 1914

## Higher It Grows
(Tune: Whiter Than Snow)

Lord Jesus, I long to be perfectly whole,
So listen to stories of you that I'm told,
But then when I do so the bullshit just flows.
I pull up my boots because higher it grows.

Lord Jesus, let nothing of my mind remain,
Except for your crap and your theories insane.
The more that I listen more garbage in blows.
Just builds up inside and so higher it grows.

Lord Jesus, look down from thy throne in the skies
And bring to my brain an early demise.
To your nonsense and your myths my mind expose,
And pile up the shit so that higher it grows.

CHORUS:
Higher it grows. Yes, higher it grows.
The bullshit piles up, and so higher it grows.

Original Words: James L. Nicholson, 1872

# Open My Eyes That I May See

Open my eyes that I may see what stupid truth thou hast for me,
How sad and dreadful your words can be, how from such folly I should flee.

Open my ears that I may hear and understand how you're so queer.
Clear up my head, and make it so clear how religion my brain does smear.

Open my mind that I may read, understand what a line you feed.
Clear up my mind, so I will be freed from hogwash like your stupid creed.

CHORUS:
Silently now I wait for thee. Hurry before my pants I pee.
Cure my religious lunacy, spirit divine!

Original Words: Clara H. Scott, 1895

# Face Disgrace
(Tune: Face to Face)

Face disgrace, that's Christ the savior. Great disgrace he'll bring to thee
When your thinking and behavior you base on his lunacy.

Face disgrace, that's what you will do when you throw your brain away
And believe in Jesus' voodoo, letting your brain cells decay.

Face disgrace, how would you like to face disgrace and ignominy.
If virtuous religion strikes you then disgraceful you will be.

CHORUS:
Face disgrace, I feel so sorry. Doesn't matter how it's sliced.
Face disgrace, that is my story when I follow Jesus Christ.

Original Words: Carrie Ellis Breck, 1898

# My Faith and Gullibility
(Tune: My Faith Looks Up to Thee)

My faith and gullibility makes me believe in thee, savior divine.
Now hear me while I pray. You cause me great dismay,
Cause my brain to decay with your dumb line.

How thy grand myths impart ideas not so smart, make me perspire.
For thou hast lied to me, taken my dignity,
Made me like a zombie -- a fate most dire.

While life's dark maze I tread your fool myths fill my head, you lousy guide.
Bid darkness turn to day, taking your lies away.
No more my mind you'll fray. Give me my pride.

Original Words: Ray Palmer, 1830

# Were You There?

Were you there when they crucified my brain? (Were you there?)
Were you there when they crucified my brain? (Were you there?)
Oh, sometimes it causes me to tremble, tremble, tremble.
Were you there when they crucified my brain? (Were you there?)

Were you there when they made me go insane? (Were you there?)
Were you there when they made me go insane? (Were you there?)
Oh, sometimes it causes me to tremble, tremble, tremble.
Were you there when they made me go insane? (Were you there?)

... they laid on me their claims? ...
... with me they did raise Cain? ...
... my intellect they drained? ...

Original Words: African-American spiritual

# Holey, Holey, Holey
(Tune: Holy, Holy, Holy)

Holey, holey, holey. All my socks are holey,
Kind of like my foolish head when I believe in thee.
Holey, holey, holey. Such my beliefs will be,
Ignoring evidence, to trust deity.

Holey, holey, holey. My shirts have at least three,
Much like all religions that deny reality.
Holey, holey, holey. That holy book is thusly,
Filled with errors, myths, and things that don't agree.

Holey, holey, holey. Holes in my pants knee.
So are the ideas that come by divine decree.
Holey, holey, holey. All religions I see
Are filled with holes, errors and deformity.

Original Words: Reginald Heber, 1826

# A Wild, Snotty Thing
(Tune: A Child of the King)

My father is rich in houses and lands.
He holdeth the wealth of the world in his hands.
And I, as his child, am a spoiled little brat.
I cause so much trouble wherever I'm at.

My father's own son, the savior of men,
Once wandered on earth trying to make mayhem,
And now he is pleading my pardon on high,
So I can continue his antics to ply.

I once was an upstanding person of earth,
A scholar by choice and a citizen by birth.
But now that I'm saved and my name's written down
I talk like a fool and behave like a clown.

CHORUS:
I'm a wild snotty thing, a wild snotty thing.
With Jesus my savior I'm a wild snotty thing.

Original Words: Hattie E. Buell, 1877

## Depraved, Depraved
(Tune: Saved, Saved)

I've found a friend who lies to me. Nothing he says is true.
Now I'll tell you the same tall story, just so I can bamboozle you.

So now I try to do as much harm as I can do each day.
I'm leaning strong on his mighty arm, so that I can naïve minds sway.

When poor and needy and all alone and weak in self-esteem,
About Jesus I will drone and drone until you succumb to my scheme.

CHORUS
Depraved by his pow'r divine. Depraved, and it's so sublime!
Life now is sweet, and my joy is complete. I'm depraved, depraved, depraved!

Original Words: Jack P. Sholfield

## Oh, Will You Feel Sorry?
(Tune: O That Will Be Glory)

When all my labors and trials are shot,
And everything I've done has gone to pot,
It just amounts to a big pile of snot,
Will you feel sorry, so sorry for me?

When in great stupidity I do place
My faith and confidence in Jesus' grace,
And then look silly with pie in my face,
Will you feel sorry, so sorry for me?

When you see me looking like a damn fool,
When I with praises of Jesus do drool,
And my brain has lost the thread from its spool
Will you feel sorry, so sorry for me?

CHORUS:
Oh, will you feel sorry for me, sorry for me, sorry for me?
When in disgrace no one do I dare face, will you feel sorry, feel sorry for me?

Original Words: Charles H. Gabriel, 1900

# Fall for Jesus
### (Tune: All for Jesus)

Fall for Jesus! Fall for Jesus! Giving up all my brain's pow'rs
So that I can live in ignorance all my days and all my hours.
[*Chorus:*] Fall for Jesus! Fall for Jesus! All my days and all my hours.
Fall for Jesus! Fall for Jesus! All my days and all my hours.

Let my hands perform his bidding. Let my feet run in his ways.
Let my eyes see Jesus only, so I'll live in a big daze.
[*Chorus:*] Fall for Jesus! Fall for Jesus! So I'll live in a big daze.
Fall for Jesus! Fall for Jesus! So I'll live in a big daze.

Since my eyes were fixed on Jesus I've lost sight of all beside.
So enchained my spirit's vision, all of my brain cells have died.
[*Chorus:*] Fall for Jesus! Fall for Jesus! All of my brain cells have died.
Fall for Jesus! Fall for Jesus! All of my brain cells have died.

Oh, what wonder! How amazing! Jesus, glorious king of kings,
Lobotomized my brain so I could be one of his ding-a-lings.
[*Chorus:*] Fall for Jesus! Fall for Jesus! Be one of his ding-a-lings.
Fall for Jesus! Fall for Jesus! Be one of his ding-a-lings.

Original Words: Mary D. James

> *With or without religion you would have good people doing good things and evil people doing evil things. But for good people to do evil things, that takes religion.*    -- Steven Weinberg

# 'Tis So Sweet to Trust in Jesus

'Tis so sweet to trust in Jesus, just to take him at his word,
Just to rest upon his promise, no matter that it's absurd.

I'm so glad I learned to trust him. No more I think for myself --
Just trust what he says is true and put my brain up on a shelf.

Oh, how sweet to trust in Jesus, just to trust his cleansing blood,
Standing proudly in his nonsense. No one knows I'm just a pud.

Yes, 'tis sweet to trust in Jesus, just from brain and sense to cease,
Rest in ignorance so bliss and not realize how I've been fleeced.

CHORUS:
Jesus, Jesus, how I trust him, since my boat is missing an oar.
Jesus, Jesus, precious Jesus! Forgive me if I start to snore.

Original Words: Louisa M. R. Stead, 1882

## Jesus, I Come

Out of my freedom, gladness and light, Jesus, I come, Jesus, I come,
Into thy bondage, sorrow and night, Jesus, I come to thee.
Out of my wellness into bad health, out of my fortune to give you my wealth,
Out of my openness into thy stealth, Jesus, I come to thee.

Out of my bathroom where I do floss, Jesus, I come, Jesus, I come,
Into the lunacy of thy cross, Jesus I come to thee.
Out of earth's spaces where I am calm into the innocent places you bomb,
Singing some verses of a dumb psalm, Jesus, I come to thee.

Out of good sense in which I have pride, Jesus, I come, Jesus, I come,
Into thy foolishness to abide, Jesus, I come to thee.
Out of myself and all of my love into despair of that god up above,
While up my ass your crap do you shove, Jesus I come to thee.

Original Words: William T. Sleeper, 1887

## Oh, Happy Day!

Oh, happy day that fixed my choice on thee, my savior and my god!
In ignorance I now rejoice and tell its raptures all so flawed.

Oh, happy bond that seals my vows to him whose fables I just love.
And now my brain is like a cow's, and up your ass his myths I'll shove.

'Tis done. The great transaction's done. I am my lord's and he is mine.
Now my brain lives down in my buns, so listen to my big ass whine.

CHORUS:
Happy day, happy day, when Jesus washed my brains away!
He taught me how to watch and pray, and live so stupid every day.
Happy day, happy day, when Jesus washed my brains away!

Original Words: Philip Doddridge, 1755

## When We All Get to Heaven

Swing those wondrous buns of Jesus. How he moves them with such grace.
When we dance with him in heaven we will sure pick up the pace.

While we walk the pilgrim pathway clouds will overspread the sky.
But to dance in Jesus' heaven we'll pirouette while eating pie.

Onward to the prize before us. Soon his rhumba we'll behold.
When he moves his hips in rhythm clap and cheer his moves so bold.

CHORUS:
When we all get to heaven we will be so damn glad our pants we'll pee.
When we all see Jesus we'll bounce up and down upon his knee.

Original Words: E. E. Hewitt, 1898

## Will You Eat Pie in the Sky?
(Tune: In the Sweet By and By)

There's a land that is fairer than day where we'll meet when our bodies are dead.
At least that is what some people say who are rather mixed up in the head.

If you trust god someday you will know such joy forevermore, so they claim.
And some people they surely will snow even though they have promises lame.

Let us promise them pie in the sky -- happiness that will not ever end.
There's no way to know until they die, so our claims we won't have to defend.

CHORUS:
Will you eat pie in the sky? Will you meet on that beautiful shore?
Will you eat pie in the sky, or do just empty promises roar?

Original Words: Sanford Fillmore Bennett, 1868

## Swing Low, Sweet Chariot

I looked over Jordan, and what did I see coming for to carry me home?
A band of angels coming after me, coming to take me to their gnome.

If you get there before I do. Coming for to carry me home.
Just tell that gnome I'm coming, too. Coming to take me to your gnome.

I'm some times up and some times down. Coming for to carry me home.
To meet that gnome I'm heavenly bound. Coming to take me to your gnome.

The damnedest day that I can say. Coming for to carry me home.
Is when that gnome takes me away. Coming to take me to your gnome.

CHORUS:
Swing low, sweet chariot, coming for to carry me home.
Swing low, sweet chariot, coming to take me to your gnome.

Original Words: Traditional spiritual

## Shall We Blather at the River
(Tune: Shall We Gather at the River)

Shall we blather at the river where cute angel feet have trod,
Marching with cute little quivers on and on droning for god.

On the margin of the river, washing up its silver spray,
Blather even as we shiver, and lots of gibberish we'll say.

Ere we reach the shining river where we really will get down
Our bunk and nonsense we'll deliver to just every naïve fool around.

Soon we'll reach the shining river. Soon our pilgrimage will cease.
To that river we will give her all the fools that we have fleeced.

CHORUS:
Yes, we'll blather at the river. We'll drivel, babble, shake and quiver.
Blather like damn fools at the river, and on we will drone for god.

Original Words: Robert Lowry, 1864

## Peas, Perfect Peas
(Tune: Peace, Perfect Peace)

Peas, perfect peas in this dark world of sin.
Eat lots of peas to give you peas within.

Peas, perfect peas in this dark world below.
Eat lots of peas to make your rosy cheeks glow.

Peas, perfect peas in a world that eats not well.
Eat peas today to have a meal right swell.

Peas, perfect peas in a world of little ease.
Get good nutrition eating nice green peas.

Peas, perfect peas in this world full of beans.
Get some good peas to eat by any means.

Peas, perfect peas. They're vegetables so small,
Like brains of those who for religion fall.

Original Words: Edward Henry Bickersteth, 1875

## Come, Thou Long-Expected Jesus

*Verily I say unto you, There be some standing here, which shall not taste of death, till they see the Son of man coming in his kingdom. - Matthew 16:28*

Come, thou long-expected Jesus, born to set thy people free.
Come and bring us lots of pizzas covered with pepperoni.
Israel's strength and consolation, hope of all the earth thou art.
Get over your constipation so you can come do your part.

Come, thou long-expected Jesus, expected for two thousand years.
If you'd show it sure would please us if you could bring a few beers.
Some who saw your tricks so fancy would see your return you said.
They are getting rather antsy. Would you please get out the lead?

Come, thou long-expected Jesus. Long ago you said you'd come.
Were you just trying to tease us. How long will you sit on your bum?
Two thousand years ago you told us your return would not be long.
Why do you in suspense hold us while you sit and play with your dong?

Original Words: Charles Wesley

## Seek Out New Temptations
### (Tune: Yield Not to Temptation)

Seek out new temptations, new chances to sin.
Each time you yield to one you earn god's chagrin.
Sin manfully onward. Dark passions enjoy.
Look ever to Jesus. He's a naughty old boy.

Love evil companions. Bad language engrain
Into you so you will take god's name in vain.
Be thoughtful and earnest. Seek new ways to sin.
When you try a new one you will walk with a grin.

At him that sins often god maketh a frown.
To see him snivel and snort is the best fun around.
Remember to go out, find temptation each day,
Yielding to it in all that you think, do or say.

CHORUS:
Ask the savior to help you, new temptations to find you,
So you'll sin in some ways new. He will find some for you.

Original Words: Horatio R. Palmer, 1868

## Haze Him! Haze Him!
### (Tune: Praise Him! Praise Him!)

Haze him! Haze him! Let's haze that brand new church member.
Make him lies and fables and myths proclaim.
Fail him! Fail him! That is what Jesus will do,
But that's alright 'cause we don't know any shame.
Like a schlepper Jesus ignores his children.
He's too busy toking on his big bong.

Haze him! Haze him! Make him get down on his knees,
And beg and grovel like a poor little fool.
Flail him! Assail him! Jump up and down on his toes.
Then slap him silly and on his jacket drool.
Before you accept him into your sacred club
Take his clothes off and dress him up in a thong.

Haze him! Haze him! Don't let him get out unscathed.
Make him stupid, nonsensical canticles sing.
Fill his head with colorful contradictions
'Til no longer does he know anything.
Take his money. Call it a freewill offering.
Make him pay your mystical cult to belong.

CHORUS:
Haze him! Haze him! Destroy his integrity.
Haze him! Haze him! Make him feel like a big dong!

Original Words: Fanny Crosby, 1869

# Blessed Quietness

Shit is flowing like a river since the Christian nuts have come.
Up my spine it sends a shiver just to hear their crap so dumb.

One day, though, we'll have such gladness when we get rid of these pests,
Be rid of all of their badness, finally have some peace and rest.

One day we'll come to our senses, toss those nuts out on their rears,
Hang them up on picket fences, tie their tongues and pull their ears.

CHORUS:
Blessed quietness, peaceful quietness, what assurance in my soul.
When the Christian nuts all their mouths have shut
We won't miss their constant droll.

Original Words: Manie P. Ferguson

---

> I've begun worshipping the sun for a number of reasons. First of all, unlike some other gods I could mention, I can see the sun. It's there for me every day. And the things it brings me are quite apparent all the time: heat, light, food, a lovely day. There's no mystery, no one asks for money, I don't have to dress up, and there's no boring pageantry. And interestingly enough, I have found that the prayers I offer to the sun and the prayers I formerly offered to God are all answered at about the same 50-percent rate.       -- George Carlin

---

# Christly Fleas!
(Tune: Christ in Me)

This is my horrible story: Fleas to my head have come.
Jesus, that villain so sorry, sent them upon me, that scum.

Oh, how those damn fleas are moving, biting and causing me pain.
And they are constantly proving Jesus is to us a bane.

No matter how I implore him Jesus won't do a thing
To end this agony sore, so all I can do now is sing:

CHORUS:
Christly fleas! Christly fleas! Christly fleas, oh, horrible story.
Christly fleas! Christly fleas! Christly fleas -- a tale so sorry.

Original Words: Albert Benjamin Simpson

# Where He Leads Me

I can hear my savior calling. I can hear my savior calling.
I can hear my savior calling. "Come and wallow. Wallow here with me."

I will wallow in his slime, I will wallow in his slime.
I will wallow in his slime. "Come and wallow. Wallow here with me."

I will wallow in his madness. I will wallow in his madness.
I will wallow in his madness. "Come and wallow. Wallow here with me."

I will wallow in obtuseness. I will wallow in obtuseness.
I will wallow in obtuseness. "Come and wallow. Wallow here with me."

CHORUS:
Where he leads me I will wallow. Where he leads me I will wallow.
Where he leads me I will wallow. I will wallow, wallow all the way.

Original Words: E. W. Blandy

> *Whenever we read the obscene stories, the voluptuous debaucheries, the cruel and tortuous executions, the unrelenting vindictiveness with which more than half the Bible is filled, it would be more consistent that we call it the word of a demon than the word of God. It is a history of wickedness that has served to corrupt and brutalize humankind.*
>
> *-- Thomas Paine*

# You Screwed My Vision
(Tune: Be Thou My Vision)

You screwed my vision, oh lord of my heart.
Why did you have to get in my face and fart?
Now I can't see things in day or in night,
Even if I carry a great big light.

You screwed my wisdom with your twisted words.
Your stupid nonsense is just for the birds.
Thou my great father -- what stupidity!
If you're my father I'll jump off a tree.

You screwed my fission, you blasted old fart!
Now I can't get this bomb I built to start.
Now how will I all my enemies dispel
And send all of their bad souls down to hell?

Original Words: Eleanor H. Hull, Mary A. Byrne (translator)

## You May Have the Joy-Smells
(Tune: You May Have the Joy-Bells)

You may have the joy-smells springing from your fart
And a smell that from you never will depart.
Swallow what we have to say. Ooze his nonsense every day.
It will keep the joy-smells springing from your fart.

Love of Jesus is illusion you may know.
So to those around you it you cannot show.
But you can swallow his crap. Let it all your brain enwrap.
Then you'll have the joy-smells springing from your fart.

You will meet with reason as you journey on.
Don't let common sense in your mind doubts then spawn.
Just accept our crock of shit down into your stomach pit.
It will keep the joy-smells springing from your fart.

CHORUS:
Joy-smells springing from your fart.
Joy-smells springing from your fart.
Eat his crap down here below, so that everywhere you go
You may have the joy-smells springing from your fart.

Original Words: J. Edward Ruark

## Ye Must Read Porn Again
(Tune: Ye Must Be Born Again)

A ruler once came to Jesus by night
To ask him the way to be cheery and bright.
The master made answer in words true and plain:
"Ye must read porn again."

Ye children of men, attend to the word,
And let all your hormones be mightily stirred.
And let not this message to you be in vain:
"Ye must read porn again."

Oh, ye who would enter that glorious state
When you are so eager to go copulate,
And if a good strong hard-on ye would obtain
Ye must read porn again.

CHORUS:
Ye must read porn again. Ye must read porn again.
I verily, verily, say unto thee, "Ye must read porn again."

Original Words: William T. Sleeper

# Part 5

## Songs for Hardcore Atheists

Don't even think of sharing these songs with your Christian friends!

# How Odd Is the Story
(Tune: To God Be the Glory)

How odd is the story of what god has done.
Created the earth and the stars, moon and sun,
And man and a woman in a garden so fair,
And then kicked them out when they ate what was there.

God made a great nation from Abraham's seed,
A man who when asked to kill his son agreed.
Twelve tribes came from Jacob, his grandson, the shrew
Who cheated his brother and blackmailed him too.

God sent them to Egypt, a nice little band,
When god sent a famine to their promised land,
Then came back and led them away from those parts.
He killed Egypt's folks, hardening Pharaoh's heart.

He led them to Canaan, a land, oh, so fair,
To find that some other people did live there.
He sent them each man, woman and child to kill
And steal their real estate his vow to fulfill.

When his dear children were not to him true
His self-righteous anger and jealousy grew.
He sent in the heathens to carry out his will,
His nation to destroy and people to kill.

So finally he sent to us Jesus his son
To save us from everything that we find fun,
To take away from us all that we do crave
And turn us all into his good little slaves.

CHORUS:
Oh my lord! Oh my lord! What a tale do they weave.
I am floored, I am floored, that they say they believe
That god is so loving, and Jesus is, too.
What happened to their brains? Did they turn to goo?

Original Words: Fanny Crosby, 1875

# How Marvelous! How Wonderful!

I stand amazed in the presence of followers of Jesus strange
And wonder how they could do it. Are they just really deranged?

For me it was in the garden. I prayed, "God, what followers thine!
They bear quite a strong resemblance to a guy named Frankenstein."

He took my sins and my sorrow. He made them his very own.
Such is the story they tell us. It tickles my funny bone.

When with great laughter and glory some Christian so duped I see
'Twill be my joy as he ages to sing of his fantasy.

CHORUS:
How marvelous! How wonderful! So this tale shall ever be.
How marvelous! How wonderful! What fantastic fantasy!

Original Words: Charles Hutchinson Gabriel, 1905

## Soldiers of Christ, Surprise!
### (Tune: Soldiers of Christ, Arise!)

Soldiers of Christ, surprise! Your fight is all in vain.
Oh, nobody your nonsense buys if he has half a brain.
We're already so full of all your crock of bull
That no longer can you the wool over our blind eyes pull.

Soldiers of Christ, surprise! Oh, it's not what you thought.
Oh, fibs and lies that god supplies are all that you have bought.
And now you get to spread your superstitions wild,
And all the nonsense in your head that your mind has defiled.

Soldiers of Christ, surprise! You're caught with your pants down.
Your asses stick out, and you guys look like a bunch of clowns.
There's not a friggin' trace of evidence to show
That your lies have any base. No, smoke is all you blow.

Soldiers of Christ, surprise! You fight a losing cause.
No thinking soul your rubbish buys. It has too many flaws.
Oh, please come down from space and put your swords away.
Come rejoin the human race and have a pleasant day.

Original Words: Charles Wesley, 1749

## More Oiliness Give Me
### (Tune: More Holiness Give Me)

More oiliness give me without and within,
So I can more smoothly god's nice fables spin.
Oil sometimes is needed to give proper care.
More oiliness give me so I'll have some to spare.

More oiliness give me, to be like the lord,
Though he is so oily and slick that he's abhorred.
His oiliness gives us a whole lot of grief.
More oiliness give me so I'll have relief.

More oiliness give me, more strength to o'ercome,
To fill lots of heads with your madness and scum.
When spreading your nonsense more useful I'd be
If I could be as smooth and oily as thee.

Original Words: P. P. Bliss

## Faith of Our Fathers

Faith of our fathers living still in spite of science, logic and sense.
Oh, what a bunch of rot and swill people will believe. Oh, how dense!

Our fathers, they lived in the dark unaware of reality.
How sweet would be their children's fate to be set from superstition free.

Faith of our fathers, we will strive to undo all the damage you've done,
To break thru all your nonsense and jive, undo the web of lies you have spun.

Faith of our fathers, no longer will we subscribe to myths and fantasy,
But will put our trust in things we can see have solid base in reality.

CHORUS:
Faith of our fathers, holy shit! It happened when their brains did quit.

Original Words: Frederick William Faber, 1849

## I Know Whom I Have Believed

I know not why god's foolish bunk to me he hath made known,
Nor why people will buy this crap. Are they dumb as a stone?

I know not how this naïve faith makes people to believe,
Nor how, with evidence not a trace, I can still people deceive.

I know not what of good or ill may be reserved for me,
Or how it is I have this skill to fool folks so handily.

CHORUS:
But I know whom I have believed and am persuaded that his nice fable
Will keep those whom I've bamboozled so confused unto the end.

Original Words: D. W. Whittle, 1883

## Count Me

When you count the ones who love the lord, count me, count me!
Who into their heads have nonsense poured, count me, count me!

When you count up those who're saved by grace, count me, count me!
Who have lost their minds without a trace, count me, count me!

When you count up those who do the right, count me, count me!
In accord with god, who's full of spite, count me, count me!

CHORUS:
Count me with the children of the heav'nly king.
Count me with the servants who to myths do cling.
Count me with the ransomed who don't know a thing.
Count me, count me!

Original Words: William C. Poole

## Nothing Between

Nothing between my right and my left ear,
Naught of intelligence or senses keen.
I accept Jesus' teaching so queer.
My right and left ears -- there's nothing between.

Nothing between my ears right and left
Since Jesus Christ attacked me so mean.
Of my intelligence I am now bereft.
My ears right and left -- there's nothing between.

Nothing between my ears left and right.
Not an intelligent thought could you glean.
Jesus has left my head not so right.
My ears left and right -- there's nothing between.

CHORUS:
Nothing between my right and my left ear,
Not since Christ Jesus wiped it right clean.
Nothing preventing believing things most queer.
Right and left ears, there's nothing between.

Original Words: Charles Albert Tindley, 1905

> *Wandering in a vast forest at night, I have only a faint light to guide me. A stranger appears and says to me, "My friend, you should blow out your candle in order to find your way more clearly." This stranger is a theologian.*     -- Denis Diderot

## Lord, I Want to Be a Christian

Lord, I want to be a Christian ina my heart, ina my heart.
Lord, I want to be a Christian ina my heart, ina my heart, ina my heart,
Lord, I want to be a Christian ina my heart.

Lord, I want to be a dimwit ina my heart, ina my heart.
Lord, I want to be a dimwit ina my heart, ina my heart, ina my heart,
Lord, I want to be a dimwit ina my heart.

Lord, I want to remain stupid ina my heart, ina my heart.
Lord, I want to remain stupid ina my heart, ina my heart, ina my heart,
Lord, I want to remain stupid ina my heart.

Lord, I want to trust in fables ina my heart, ina my heart.
Lord, I want to trust in fables ina my heart, ina my heart, ina my heart,
Lord, I want to trust in fables ina my heart.

Original Words: African-American spiritual

## Just As I Am

Just as I am, without one flea, because I bathed just recently.
I used soap on my whole body. Oh, lamb of god, I come, I come.

Just as I am, though tossed about so goddamn hard I banged my snout.
Now I look like a fucking trout. Oh, lamb of god, I come, I come.

Just as I am, so wretched, blind, and, what is more, I've lost my mind.
Now even while my teeth I grind, oh, lamb of god, I come, I come.

Just as I am, thou wilt receive me as I drool upon my sleeve.
Now, as my urges I relieve, oh, lamb of god, I come, I come.

Original Words: Charlotte Elliott

## Saved! Saved! Saved!

Saved! Saved! Saved! My sins are all forgiv'n.
Let's sin more along our way to heav'n.
I was lost in all my sinful ways.
Now I've found that that's the way to play.

Saved! Saved! Saved! By grace and grace alone.
Now my mind, it has been turned to bone.
Once I used to think and use my brain.
Now to think would just be too much strain.

Saved! Saved! Saved! Oh, joy beyond compare!
Don't know a thing, but now I just don't care.
Yielding all and trusting him alone.
Living now each moment like a drone.

CHORUS:
Saved! I'm saved through Christ, my all in all.
Saved! I'm saved. No need to think at all.
He emptied out my brain, you see. He gave me a lobotomy,
And now I'm dumb eternally. I'm saved, saved, saved!

Original Words: Oswald J. Smith

## Thrust All the Way
### (Tune: Trust and Obey)

When we walk with the lord and we tend to get bored,
What a glory to find someone to lay.
As we screw with good skill, not a drop will we spill,
Just as long as we thrust all the way.

Not a shadow can rise, but when we open our flies
Something else may stand up right away.
Not a doubt or a fear, not a sigh nor a tear,
Can abide while we thrust all the way.

Not a burden we bear, not a sorrow we share,
While we romp and we roll in the hay.
Not a grief nor a loss, not a frown nor look cross,
Can appear while we thrust all the way.

CHORUS:
Thrust all the way, for there's no other way
To have a real good climax, but to thrust all the way.

Original Words: John H. Sammis, 1887

## Come, Thou Mount of Shit Distressing
(Tune: Come, Thou Fount of Every Blessing)

Come, thou mount of shit distressing, do you think we buy your crap?
With our minds you're always messing. Try to draw us to your trap.
Let us draw our boots up high as your crap flows wide and deep.
Grab our shovels. Try not to sigh as it's piled in a big heap.

Come, thou mount of shit distressing, you sure are a great disgrace.
With your lies you're always pressing, trying to our minds debase.
With your myths and superstitions you amaze us every day.
All your blunders, contradictions your great ignorance do convey.

Come, thou mount of shit distressing, will you always carry on
Trying to put window dressing on your blunders and your con?
Seeking always to bamboozle all of those whose minds are weak.
Try to turn their brains to strudel, confuse with the double speak.

Original Words: Robert Robinson 1758; Martin Madan 1760

## Love Divine, Your Butt Is Smelling
(Tune: Love Divine, All Loves Excelling)

Love divine, your butt is smelling. Stench of heaven to earth come down,
Get out of my humble dwelling and go wash your ass so brown.
Jesus, show us some compassion if unbounded love thou art.
Bear yourself in kindly fashion. Do not in our presence fart.

Love divine, your butt is smelling. It's been stinking far too long,
Wreaking strong, its odor swelling, wafting odor foul and strong.
Jesus, please go take a shower. Wash real good that smelly rear.
Scrub it hard with lots of power before you again come near.

Love divine, your butt is smelling. Spreading stench through all the world.
Grievous odor you're expelling, noxious gas against us hurled.
Jesus, will you wash your rear end? Make it clean and odor free.
Bring it right up to first class so we can all breathe easily.

Original Words: Charles Wesley, 1747

## Sunshine on My Pole
(Tune: Sunshine in the Soul)

There is sunshine on my pole today more glorious and bright
Than glows in any earthly sky, for Jesus is my light.

There is sunshine on my pole today, for when the lord is near
His light shines brightly on my pole and make me feel right queer.

There is sunshine on my pole today. It tans up nice and brown.
When I show it to my Jesus fair his brightness shines right down.

CHORUS:
Oh, there's sunshine, blessed sunshine when the peaceful, happy moments roll.
When Jesus shows his smiling face there is sunshine on my pole.

Original Words: E. E. Hewitt

## Christ the Lord, He Isn't Too Gay
(Tune: Christ the Lord Is Risen Today)

Christ the lord, he isn't too gay. Alleluia!
Only if women he can't lay. Alleluia!
Or if he's doped up too high, Alleluia!
Can't tell a woman from a guy. Alleluia!

Christ the Lord, he isn't too gay. Alleluia!
Prefers a woman any day. Alleluia!
But if a woman he can't find, Alleluia!
He'll take one of any kind. Alleluia!

Christ the Lord, he isn't too gay. Alleluia!
Prefers a woman for his play. Alleluia!
But if worse does come to worse, Alleluia!
To enjoy a man he's not adverse. Alleluia!

Original Words: Charles Wesley, 1739

## Arise, My Pole, Arise
(Tune: Arise, My Soul, Arise)

Arise, my pole, arise! Oh, shake and jump with cheers.
A creamy white liquid, it suddenly appears.
Stiff as a bone it surely stands. Stiff as a bone it surely stands.
Just see how much that it expands.

Arise, my pole, arise! Oh, stand up proud and tall.
With bursting energy you rise to nature's call.
Oh, would you like my pole to ride? Oh, would you like my pole to ride?
Oh, get it all the way inside.

Original Words: Charles Wesley, 1742

# Oh, God Has Felt the Sage's Ass
(Tune: O God, Our Help in Ages Past)

Oh, god has felt the sage's ass and now is ready to come.
About to shoot a great big blast upon that sage's bum.

Oh, god has felt the sage's ass. It's nice and soft and warm.
Indeed his ass is just first-class. Around it angels swarm.

Oh, god has felt the sage's ass. His hand is on it still.
Since he made his very first pass it gives him a big thrill.

Oh, god has felt the sage's ass, and all his body, too.
And though you think he's being crass he'll do the same to you.

Original Words: Isaac Watts, 1719

# All the Way My Savior Leads Me

All the way my savior leads me. In his room he said to hide.
Oh god, grant me tender mercy. To be good I really tried.
He said he would give me comfort if I'd share his bed so swell.
Didn't know he would make me go all the way under his spell.
Didn't know he would make me go all the way under his spell.

All the way my savior leads me. To his chambers I do tread.
Gives me flattery and kisses as he lays me on his bed.
Yes, my weary steps may falter, and my soul corrupts does he.
Gushing from the cock before me, lo, a spring of joy I see.
Gushing from the cock before me, lo, a spring of joy I see.

All the way my savior leads me making promises of love.
All his love to me he promised climbing on me from above.
Would have saved myself for marriage, been pure on my wedding day,
But he took advantage of me and made me go all the way.
But he took advantage of me and made me go all the way.

Original Words: Fanny Crosby, 1875

# Part 6

## Christmas Non-Carols

Christmas carols rewritten to have fun with the "message of Christmas".

# The First "Oh, Hell!"
## (Tune: The First Noel)

The first "Oh Hell!" the angels did say
Was to certain poor shepherds in fields as they lay.
They swooped to the ground right near the sheep
And landed in a pile of sheep shit so deep.
"Oh hell! Oh hell! Oh hell! Oh hell!
We stepped in some fresh shit and, oh, does it smell!"

They looked up and saw a star
Shining in the east beyond them far.
It flashed across the sky. 'Twas a meteorite.
It landed on one of them, causing great fright.
"Oh hell! Oh hell! Oh hell! Oh hell!
One of us is dead and the others are not well."

Because of the light of that same star
Then three drunk men came from a village not far.
To see what had happened was their intent,
But with them they brought a terrible scent.
"Oh hell! Oh hell! Oh hell! Oh hell!
Oh, why did these drunkards have to come here and smell?"

The angels then drew up to the northwest,
And in Bethlehem they took a rest.
There they found a babe, asleep in the hay.
They started to sneeze and so they could not stay.
"Oh hell! Oh hell! Oh hell! Oh hell!
Our hay fever makes us feel misera-'bell'."

They started to leave but tripped on a lamb
And knocked over the cradle which fell with a bam!
Poor Mary screamed, "What'd you do to my kid?
You banged up his nose. Now he looks like a squid."
"Oh hell! Oh hell! Oh hell! Oh hell!
His nose is all red and it's starting to swell."

They picked up the cradle, then took to the air,
And flew fast as they could away from there.
But in their haste they forgot one thing.
One angel in his hand did the cradle still cling.
"Oh hell! Oh hell! Oh hell! Oh hell!
We've kidnapped the king of Israel."

They went back to Mary, to her mercy appealed,
"If you won't tell god then we'll make you a deal.
Each December twenty-fifth your image we'll display.
All the people will gawk and call it Christmas day.
Oh hell! Oh hell! Oh hell! Oh hell!
No one will know the truth. A tall tale we'll sell!"

Original Words: Unknown

## What Child Is This

What child is this, who, laid to rest, on Mary's lap is sleeping,
Whom angels greet with smelly feet while over his bed they are leaping?

Why lies he in such mean estate, where ox and ass are feeding?
Oh, could it be that this story is a little bit misleading?

So bring him incense, gold and myrrh, oh, three nice gifts to please him.
The myrrh he'll hold while you plate him with gold and then with the frankin-
    cense tease him.

CHORUS:
This, this is Christ, the king. Oh, shepherds gawk asking, "What's this thing?"
Haste, haste, eggs at him to fling, the babe the son of Mary.

Original Words: William Chatterton Dix, c.1868


And, of course, if you prefer, you can simply sing the original words to the previous tune:

## Greensleeves

Alas, my love, you do me wrong, to cast me off discourteously.
For I have loved you well and long, delighting in your company.

Your vows you've broken, like my heart. Oh, why did you so enrapture me?
Now I remain in a world apart, but my heart remains in captivity.

I have been ready at your hand, to grant whatever you would crave,
I have both wagered life and land, your love and goodwill for to have.

If you intend thus to disdain, it does the more enrapture me,
And even so, I still remain a lover in captivity.

My men were clothed all in green, and they did ever wait on thee;
All this was gallant to be seen, and yet thou wouldst not love me.

Thou couldst desire no earthly thing, but still thou hadst it readily.
Thy music still to play and sing; and yet thou wouldst not love me.

Well, I will pray to God on high, that thou my constancy mayst see,
And that yet once before I die, thou wilt vouchsafe to love me.

Ah, Greensleeves, now farewell, adieu, to God I pray to prosper thee,
For I am still thy lover true. Come once again and love me.

Chorus:
Greensleeves was all my joy. Greensleeves was my delight.
Greensleeves was my heart of gold, and who but my lady Greensleeves.

Author Unknown

## Don't Rest Ye Weary Gentlemen
(Tune: God Rest Ye Merry Gentlemen)

Don't rest ye weary gentlemen; go shop and spend and pay.
Buy lots of useless junk and crap to give on Christmas Day.
We must consume, consume, consume; you know this is our way,

Our kids you know they need a brand new batch of plastic toys,
So they can show them proudly to the other girls and boys,
And then have lots of stuff that they can damage and destroy.

Aunt Mary, she's the sweetest kind. We all adore her so.
We'll get her something spiffy that to all her friends she'll show.
Oh, when she shows it off just think of how her face will glow!

And cousin Janet needs some shoes to add onto her pile,
For all the old ones that she has are surely out of style.
We'll get her plastic Gucci boots; that's sure to bring a smile.

Oh, Uncle Ben has everything a guy could ever need,
But we could buy a silly tie or book he'll never read,
Or maybe he'd look awesome in pajamas made of tweed,

Cousin George we love so well. We must not forget him.
We'll buy him something classy he can wear down to the gym.
If he don't like it he can pass it off on Cousin Tim.

Mom and pop, what can we do to liven up their day?
Give them stuff they'll never need -- that will our love convey.
Useless junk will fill their lives, you know that is our way.

That's not enough we need to go and spend out even more.
Aha! Let's go and spend out some more money on the poor.
We'll buy them some more useless crap. Their real needs we'll ignore.

CHORUS:
For having lots of stuff will give us comfort and joy (comfort and joy).
Lots of stuff will give us comfort and joy.

Original Words: Traditional English carol

> *The way to see by Faith is to shut the Eye of Reason.*
> *-- Benjamin Franklin*

> *If God really existed, it would be necessary to abolish him.*
> *-- Mikhail Bakunin*

## While Shepherds Watched Their Flocks

While shepherds watched their flocks by night all seated on the ground
An angel of the lord came down, and glory shone around,
And glory shone around.

"Fear not," said he. "Don't let my dread upset your troubled minds."
And then he did the angel dance with lots of bumps and grinds,
With lots of bumps and grinds.

"To you, in David's town," he said, "is born of David's line
A little child around whose birth a grand hoax we'll design,
A grand hoax we'll design."

"The witless babe you there shall find to human view displayed,
All simply wrapped in swaddling clothes, his face with Cheez-Whiz sprayed,
His face with Cheez-Whiz sprayed."

Thus spoke the angel. Suddenly appeared a whining throng
Of drunken men, each one pie-eyed and toking on his bong,
And toking on his bong.

"All glory be to god on high," they joined in joyous song.
"To those on whom his favor rests he'll give nice new bong,
He'll give a nice new bong."

Original Words: Nahum Tate, 1700

## Listen Heavens, and I Will Speak
### (Tune: Deck the Halls)

Listen heavens. I will speak, Fa la la la la, la la la la.
Of our god; he's such a freak. Fa la la la la, la la la la.
He brought us from Egypt land, Fa la la la la, la la la la.
Killed them dead. It sure was grand! Fa la la la la, la la la la.

God is with us day and night, Fa la la la la, la la la la.
Ready always to kill and smite. Fa la la la la, la la la la.
Follow his rules; they're good for you. Fa la la la la, la la la la.
They'll sure turn your brain to goo! Fa la la la la, la la la la.

Go and meet those other races. Fa la la la la, la la la la.
Kill them dead in all their places. Fa la la la la, la la la la.
Moms and dads and kids we'll kill. Fa la la la la, la la la la.
Stone them dead -- it's such a thrill. Fa la la la la, la la la la.

Bring him rams and bulls and sheep. Fa la la la la, la la la la.
Burn them up god's cool to keep. Fa la la la la, la la la la.
If you disobey his rules. Fa la la la la, la la la la.
Seething vengeance he will drool. Fa la la la la, la la la la.

Original Words: Traditional

## Joy to the World

Joy to the world, the lord's a bum -- a really useless thing.
He holds up in his hideaway, just playing with himself all day.
So we'll go out and sing and have a happy fling.
So we'll go out and sing and have a happy fling.

Joy to the world, the savior's lame. Let men their songs employ,
And women sing along for fun, how such fool crap we'll surely shun.
Oh, reason we'll deploy, and then we'll jump for joy.
Oh, reason we'll deploy, and then we'll jump for joy.

No more let superstition grow, nor lies infest the earth.
We'll challenge those who feel they must in myths and fables put their trust.
Use brains for what they're worth and then join us in our mirth,
Use brains for what they're worth and join us in our mirth.

Original Words: Isaac Watts, 1719

## Soy to the World
(Tune: Joy to the World)

Soy to the world, so good for you. From the earth its plants will spring.
Let every house prepare tofu, and health gurus will sing,
And health gurus will sing, and health, and health gurus will sing.

Soy to the world! Where'er it rains let men their hoes employ.
In fields and pots, gardens and plains, replant those seeds of soy,
Replant those seeds of soy, replant, replant those seeds of soy.

No more let favas and limas grow, nor peas infest the ground.
We'll cultivate soy, in row by row, far as good soil is found,
Far as good soil is found, far as, far as good soil is found.

Original Words: Isaac Watts, 1719

## Angels From the Realms of Glory

Angels from the realms of glory, wing your flight o'er all the earth.
Ye who sang creation's story now proclaim the new thing's birth.

Shepherds in the field abiding watching o'er your flocks by night,
Too late now to go to hiding. Now you're part of this great fright.

Sages, leave your contemplations. Our hoax beats your dreams by far.
Spread our scam to all the nations. Someday Jesus will be a star.

CHORUS:
Drum the birth shit. Thrum the birth shit -- birth shit of that Jesus thing.

Original Words: James Montgomery, 1816

## Oh, Little Town of Bethlehem

Oh, little town of Bethlehem, how still we see thee lie!
Above thy deep and dreamless sleep the silent stars go by.
Yet in thy dark streets starteth the most outrageous hoax
That thru the years delights the ears of poor, deluded folks.

For Christ is born of Mary, and gathered all around,
While mortals sleep, the angels peek at that which does astound.
For people will proclaim that this is a holy birth,
Do anything their hoax to spring on folks throughout the earth.

Now, Joseph he was worried that his virgin was defiled.
So waxing bold Joseph she told that it was god's own child.
Then Joseph bought this story, a naïve little nerd,
And so began the biggest scam the world has ever heard.

Original Words: Phillips Brooks, 1868

## Oh, Holy Cripe!
(Tune: O, Holy Night)

Oh, holy cripe! The fools are loudly whining.
It is the night of the queer savior's birth.
Long in great ignorance have they been pining.
Now they want to spread their fib through the earth.
At such a fib the simple mind rejoices,
For on this dark night, such a tale is born --
A tale of such gay, sweet-singing angel voices.
What enticing tale, even better than porn.
What enticing tale, even better than porn.

Led by the blindness of faith gullibly beaming
With naïve hearts by his cradle we stand.
Look up! We see some fools frothing and screaming.
Here come the witless men from Orient land.
The thing it springs up from its lowly manger,
Attacks them each one, whether foe or friend.
No one can help, not whether kin nor stranger.
Oh, no person from his onslaught can defend.
Oh, no person from his onslaught can defend.

Then he grew up and said, "Love one another,"
That we should all live together in peace.
Just preach the hoax to each sister and brother,
That they from thinking and reason should cease.
Sweet hymns of joy in lame-brained chorus raise we.
Let all of us laugh at his funny name:
Christ the lord. Oh, what a scam so crazy.
Oh, everywhere this ruse we will proclaim.
Oh, everywhere this ruse we will proclaim.

Original Words: Placide Cappeau, 1847 (John S. Dwight, translator)

# The Twelve Weeks of Sunday School
(Tune: The Twelve Days of Christmas)

The first week of Sunday school my teacher said to me some garbage about a fairy.

The second week of Sunday school my teacher said to me two myths absurd I love, and some garbage about a fairy.

The third week of Sunday school my teacher said to me three French kisses, two myths absurd I love, and some garbage about a fairy.

The fourth week of Sunday school my teacher said to me four appalling words, three French kisses, two myths absurd I love, and some garbage about a fairy.

The fifth week of Sunday school my teacher said to me five bold fibs, four appalling words, three French kisses, two myths absurd I love, and some garbage about a fairy.

The sixth week of Sunday school my teacher said to me six fleeces saying ...

| | |
|---|---|
| seventh | seven cons a spinning |
| eighth | eight fables bilking |
| ninth | nine tales fancy |
| tenth | ten words deceiving |
| eleventh | eleven hypes a piping |
| twelfth | twelve rumblings dumber |

Original Words: Traditional

# We Three Kings of Orient Are

We three kings of Orient are. Like damn fools we traverse afar.
Over mountain, puds we're poundin', following yonder star.

Born a king on Bethlehem's plain. Gold I bring because I'm inane.
Not so clever, thinking never, don't want to strain my brain.

Frankincense to offer have I. Mary will bake a frankincense pie.
Bake it lightly, brown it slightly, all for the little guy.

Myrrh is mine, its bitter perfume for Jesus to smell up his room.
Under bed, and some on bread to drive away all the gloom.

CHORUS:
Oh, star of wonder, star of night. For wise men we're not so bright.
Westward leading, people greeting,
    (1.) telling us "Go fly a kite!"
    (2.) We sure are an ugly sight.
    (3.) Filling up on Miller's light.
    (4.) Find us some young child to bite.

Original Words: John H. Hopkins, 1857

# Oh, Come All Ye Mindless
### (Tune: O Come All Ye Faithful)

Oh, come, all ye mindless, joyful and moronic.
Oh, come ye, oh, come ye to Bethlehem.
Come and behold him, born to serve us bagels.

Sing, choirs of morons. Sing imagination.
Oh, sing, all ye citizens of asylums insane.
Glory to god, oh, fill him up with high test.

Yea, lord, we greet thee, born this happy morning.
Jesus to thee be a big horsie giv'n.
Will his real father be in the flesh appearing?

CHORUS:
Oh, come, let us adore him. Oh, listen to him snorin'.
Oh, cutest little foreskin. Christ, so bored.

Original Words: John Francis Wade; translated Frederick Oakeley, 1841

# Go Tell It on the Mountain

While shepherds kept their watching o'er silent flocks by night
They got all drunk and rowdy and got into a fight.

They ran off to the village of Bethlehem nearby,
Where coming from a manger they heard a baby cry.

They ran into the manger and saw the Christ-child dear,
Who scared them all right sober, because he looked so queer.

Then after that the shepherds no longer tried to fight,
Because compared to Jesus there was no greater fright.

CHORUS:
Go, tell it on the mountain, over the hills and everywhere.
Go, tell it on the mountain that Jesus Christ is born.

Original Words: African-American spiritual

# Silent Night

Silent night, holy night. All is calm. All is bright.
Round yon virgin, no longer a child. Show her a time that is wicked and wild.
She sure is quite a piece. She sure is quite a piece.

Silent night, holy night. Manliness quivers at the sight.
An angel fell from heaven afar into my bed, oh hallelujah!
In nine months a child is born. In nine months a child is born.

Silent night, holy night. Son of a bitch, she sure is tight.
Gasps of delight from her pretty face. She takes it in sport as I pick up the pace.
In nine months is a new birth. In nine months is a new birth.

Original Words: Joseph Mohr, trans: John F. Young

# Hark! The Herald Angels Stink
(Tune: Hark! The Herald Angels Sing)

Hark! The herald angels stink. Glory to the newborn fink!
Peace on earth and mercy mild, but who is this funny child?
Joyful, all ye skeptics rise. The lies they tell us we surmise.
With the thinking few proclaim: "This whole story is so lame!"

Christ by gullible dupes adored. Christ the overbearing lord!
Brain-dead eyes behold him come, queer as heck, numb as a thumb.
Open up your eyes and see absurdness and stupidity.
God comes down with man to dwell. What a story they would sell!

Hail the vaunted prince of peace! The usage of your brains now cease!
Light and life they say he brings, so why wars from religion spring?
Fight for... o-oh, Who knows why? Just so many more may die.
Born to fool the sons of earth to think they'll have a second birth.

CHORUS:
Hark! The herald angels stink. Glory to the newborn fink!

Original Words: Charles Wesley, 1739

# Part 7

## Original Music by the Author

Just so that you don't think that the only thing I know how to do is butcher and mutilate other peoples' songs!

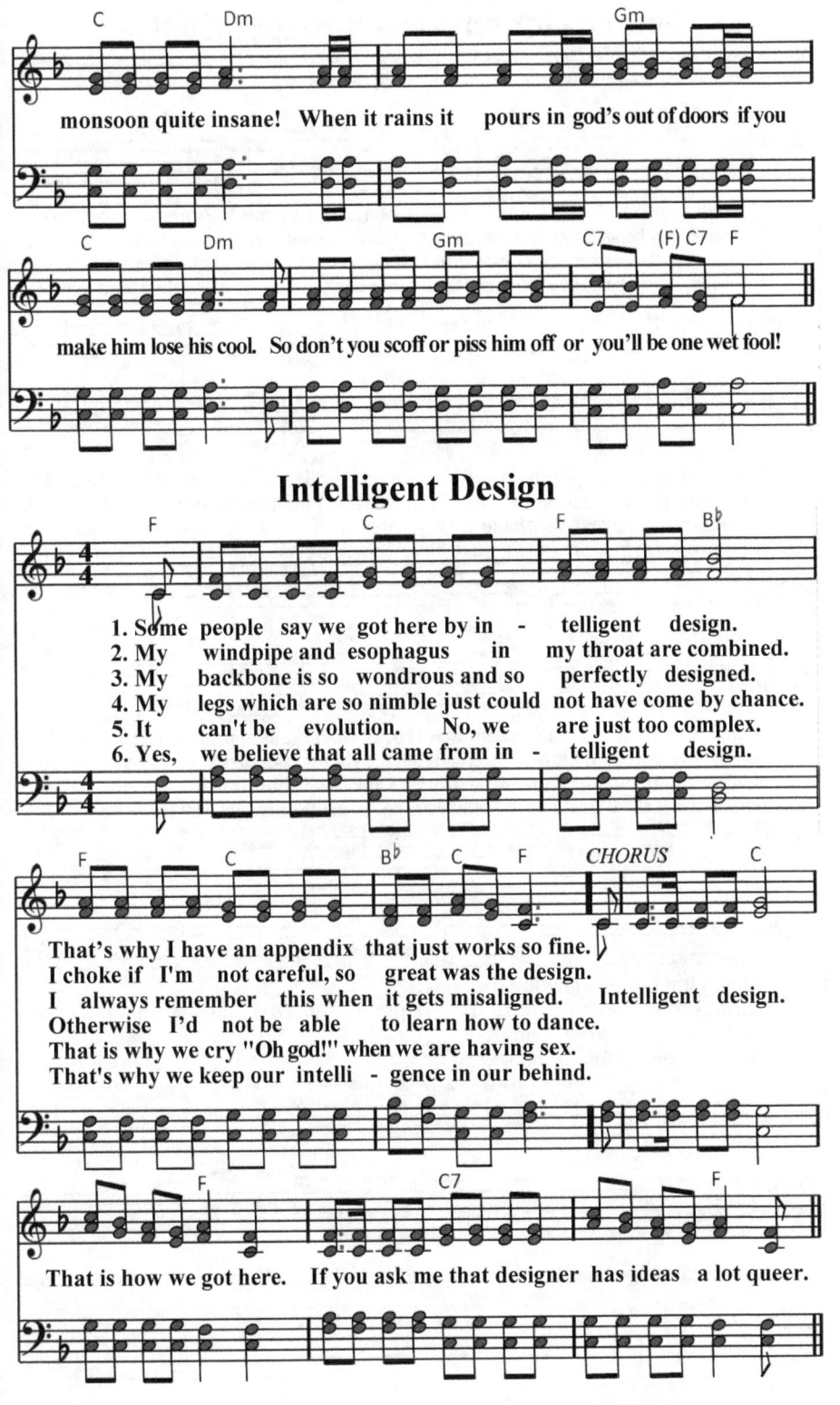

monsoon quite insane! When it rains it pours in god's out of doors if you make him lose his cool. So don't you scoff or piss him off or you'll be one wet fool!

## Intelligent Design

1. Some people say we got here by in - telligent design.
2. My windpipe and esophagus in my throat are combined.
3. My backbone is so wondrous and so perfectly designed.
4. My legs which are so nimble just could not have come by chance.
5. It can't be evolution. No, we are just too complex.
6. Yes, we believe that all came from in - telligent design.

*CHORUS*

That's why I have an appendix that just works so fine.
I choke if I'm not careful, so great was the design.
I always remember this when it gets misaligned. Intelligent design.
Otherwise I'd not be able to learn how to dance.
That is why we cry "Oh god!" when we are having sex.
That's why we keep our intelli - gence in our behind.

That is how we got here. If you ask me that designer has ideas a lot queer.

# You're Gonna Need a Bigger Boat

*Of clean beasts, and of beasts that are not clean, and of fowls, and of every thing that creepeth upon the earth, [t]here went in two and two unto Noah into the ark, the male and the female, as God had commanded Noah. -- Genesis 7:8-9*

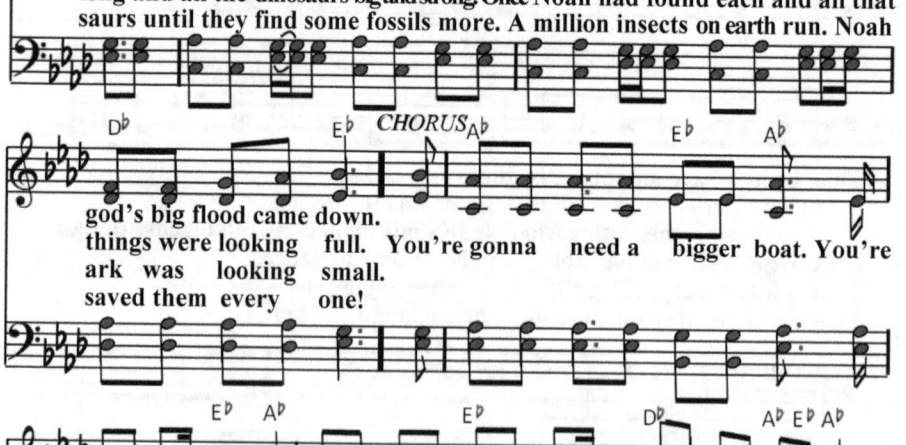

1. Noah was a holy man and built a boat, oh so grand. Four hundred fifty feet in length with gopher wood for strength. He built according to god's word, even if it did seem absurd, to hold the animals safe and sound when god's big flood came down.
2. Two of every beast he found. Could not let any of them drown. He brought them in female and male, both big or small and frail. The pigs and horses, dogs and cats, the chimps and hippos, doves and bats, the rhinos, elephants, cow and bull. Now things were looking full.
3. Then came mammoths, mastodons; then lions and tigers tagged along, giraffes and ibex, cougars too, great sloths and tiny shrews, Ti-ta-nosaur one hundred feet long and all the dinosaurs big and strong. Once Noah had found each and all that ark was looking small.
4. Five thousand mammals live today, and many more, extinct are they. Ten thousand bird kinds now are known. More in the past have flown. Seven hundred species of dinosaurs until they find some fossils more. A million insects on earth run. Noah saved them every one!

CHORUS: You're gonna need a bigger boat. You're gonna need a bigger boat. If you want that thing to float you're gonna need a bigger boat.

# Don't Spill the Seed!

*[W]hen he went in unto his brother's wife, that he spilled it on the ground, lest that he should give seed to his brother. And the thing which he did displeased the LORD: wherefore he slew him also. -- Genesis 38:9-10*

1. Er and Onan were two of Judah's kids. Er was a bad guy so god just did him in. Onan's job was to give Er's widow a child. So he went right in pre-pared to screw her wild.
2. When ready to shoot his sperm in her mound he pulled right out and he spilled it on the ground. When god saw this he was really, really mad. Onan, he then said, was very, very bad.
3. "I won't put up with that," god said. "No way!" And so he quickly struck Onan dead that day. So then when you go to have a screw, my friend, Don't pull it back out or god you will offend.

*CHORUS*

Don't spill the seed! Don't spill the seed! Be sure to keep it in. Don't pull out and sin. Never dump it on the skin. Don't spill the seed! Don't spill the seed! Don't spill the seed! Don't spill the seed! Don't spill the seed!

> The clarity of religious faith: If your child dies at the hands of a suicide bomber, it's god testing your faith. Or maybe punishing your lack of it. Or maybe he can't interfere with the bomber's free will. Or maybe he wanted the child in heaven with him. Or maybe the child was a sinner. Or maybe the child's ancestors were sinners. Or maybe god is acting in mysterious ways. Or maybe it's the work of the devil. Or maybe you worship the wrong god. Or maybe he agrees with the bomber's politics. Or maybe it's part of some great scheme. Or maybe the child was an unbeliever. Etc.,etc.,etc...
> The clarity of atheism: If your child dies when a suicide bomber blows himself up, it's because of religion.
> -- Alan Harvey

> Religion is excellent stuff for keeping common people quiet.            -- Napoleon Bonaparte

# Rex, Rex, the Dinosaur

Every day that passed they had more and more fun.

## Ha, Ha, Pharaoh!

*Then sang Moses and the children of Israel this song unto the LORD, and spake, saying, I will sing unto the LORD, for he hath triumphed gloriously: the horse and his rider hath he thrown into the sea. -- Exod. 15:1*

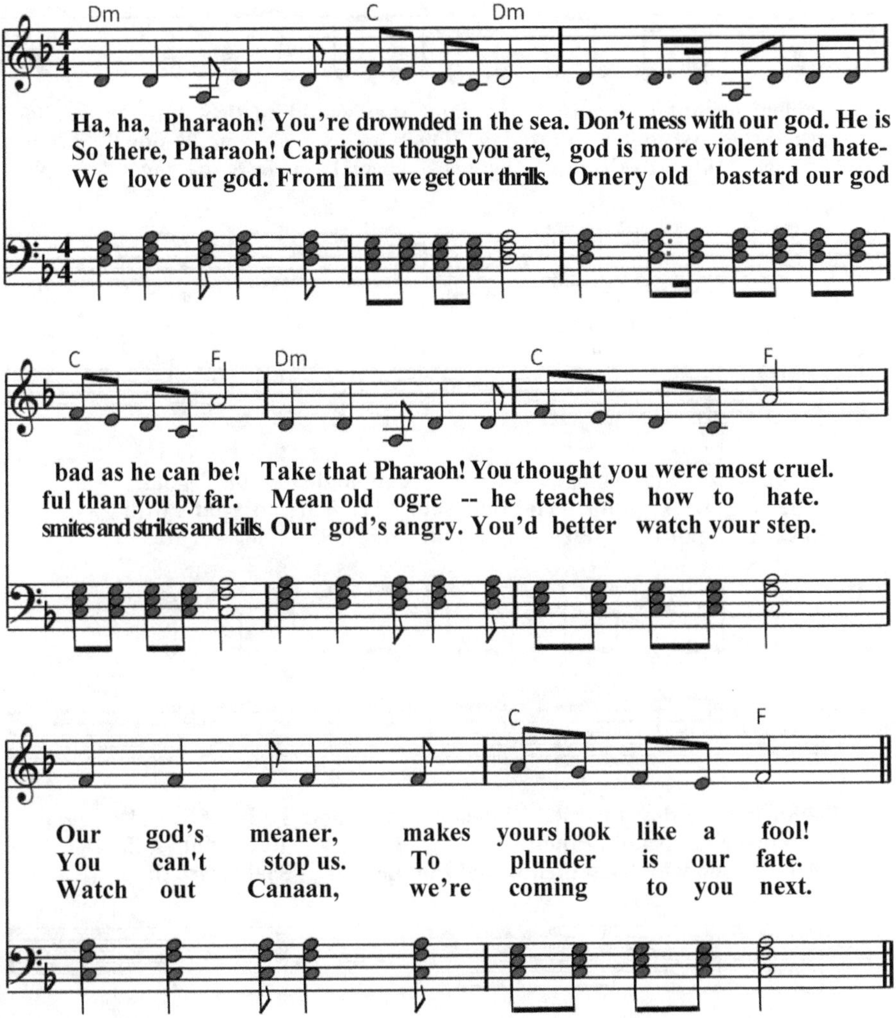

Ha, ha, Pharaoh! You're drownded in the sea. Don't mess with our god. He is
So there, Pharaoh! Capricious though you are, god is more violent and hate-
We love our god. From him we get our thrills. Ornery old bastard our god

bad as he can be! Take that Pharaoh! You thought you were most cruel.
ful than you by far. Mean old ogre -- he teaches how to hate.
smites and strikes and kills. Our god's angry. You'd better watch your step.

Our god's meaner, makes yours look like a fool!
You can't stop us. To plunder is our fate.
Watch out Canaan, we're coming to you next.

> *Why should I allow that same God to tell me how to raise my kids, who had to drown his own?*
> -- Robert G. Ingersoll

> *Religion is regarded by the common people as true, by the wise as false, and by rulers as useful.*
> -- Seneca the Younger

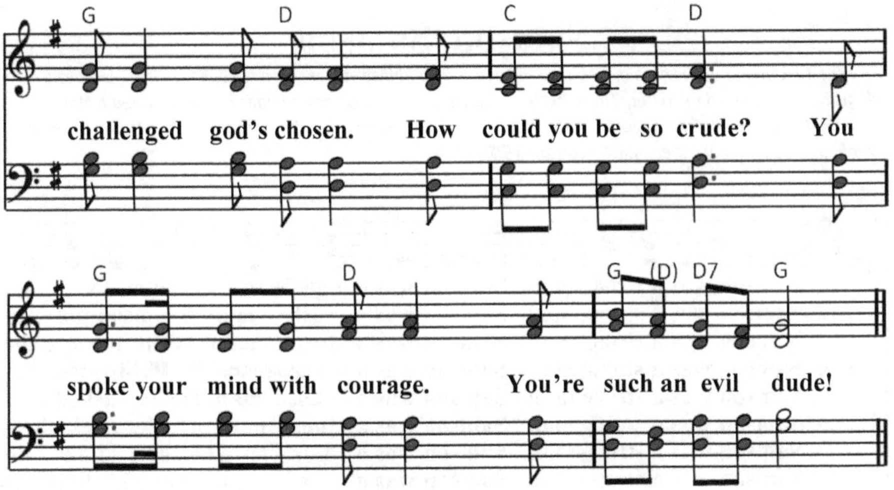

challenged god's chosen. How could you be so crude? You spoke your mind with courage. You're such an evil dude!

## Shut Up Inside the Church!

1. The church of god, oh what a place. Dis-crimin-ation women face.
2. The church of Christ is man's domain. Yes, Paul's letters make it so plain.
3. The women are just not allowed to ever preach or speak out loud.
4. So if you are of female birth the next time that you are in church

Not everyone is the same, especially if you're a dame.

*CHORUS*

"Suffer not women to speak." No, just shut up. Your sex is weak! Shut up inside the church.
They must keep their mouths shut tight, must just sit down and their tongues bite.
Be sure to keep that tongue in. Just shut that mouth and do not sin!

Do not men's place usurp. Women are second class. Shut up and sit on your ass!

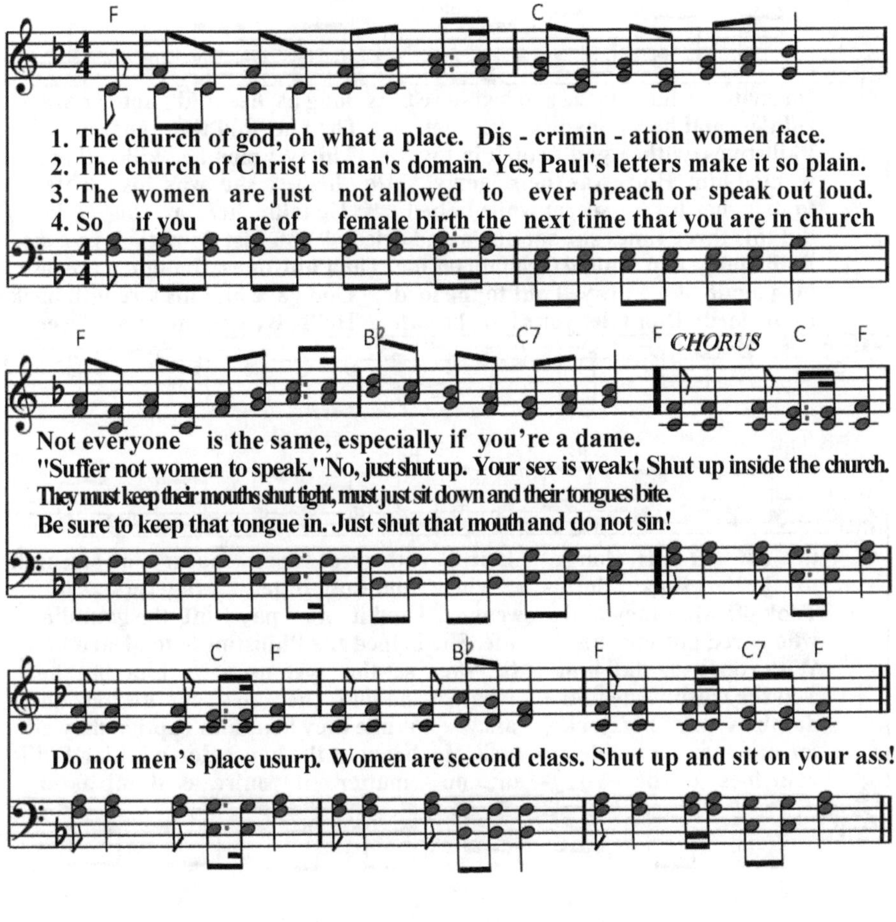

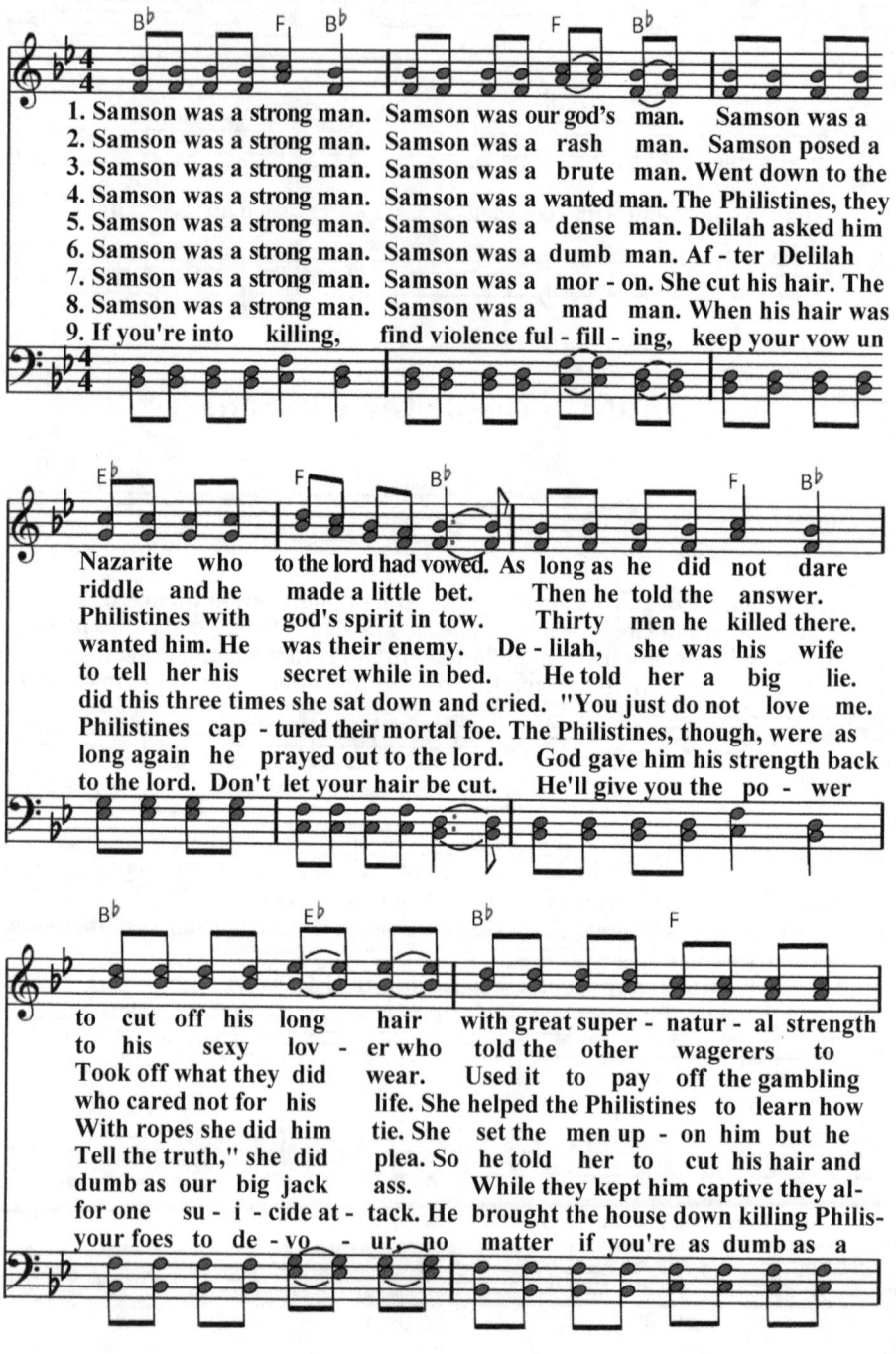

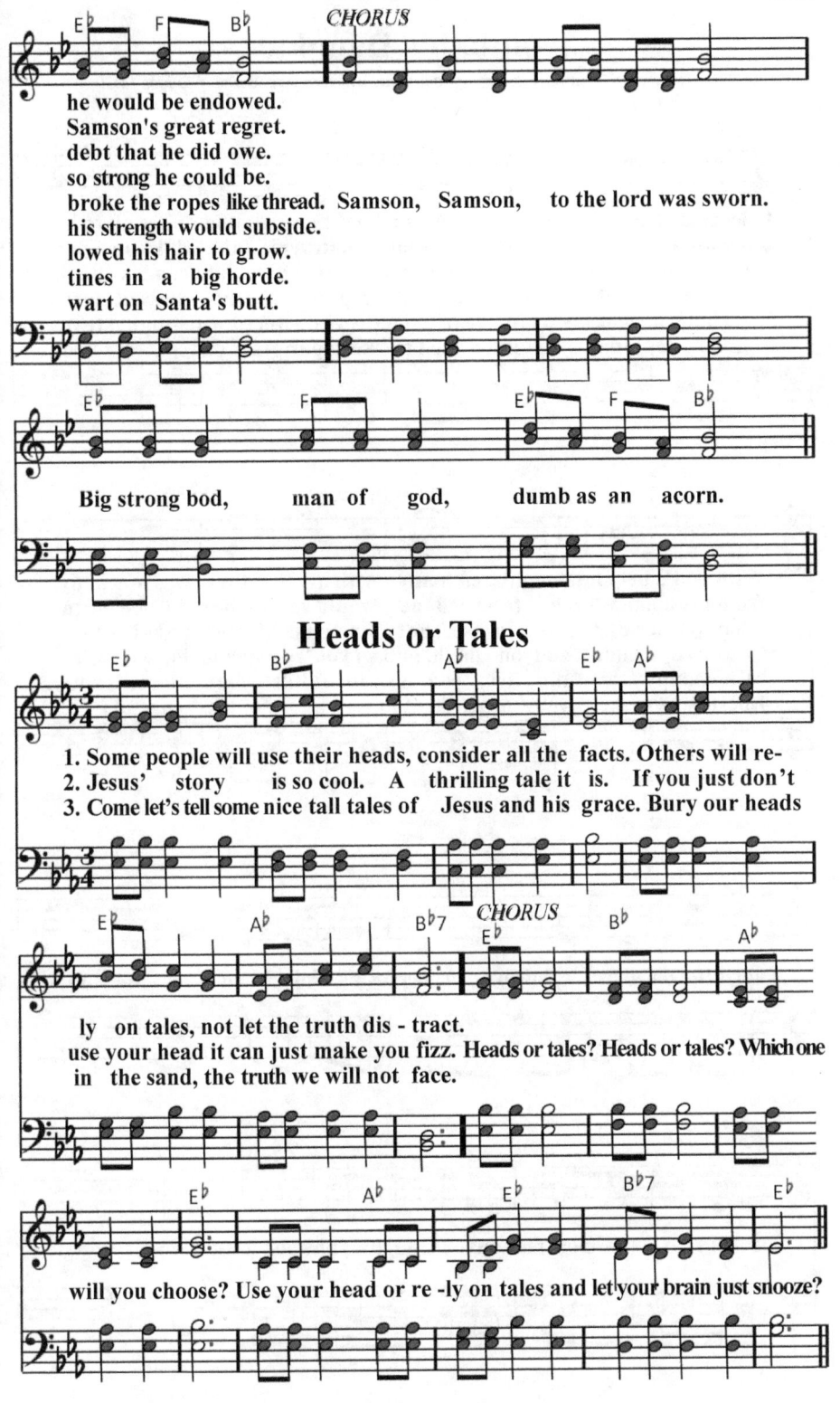

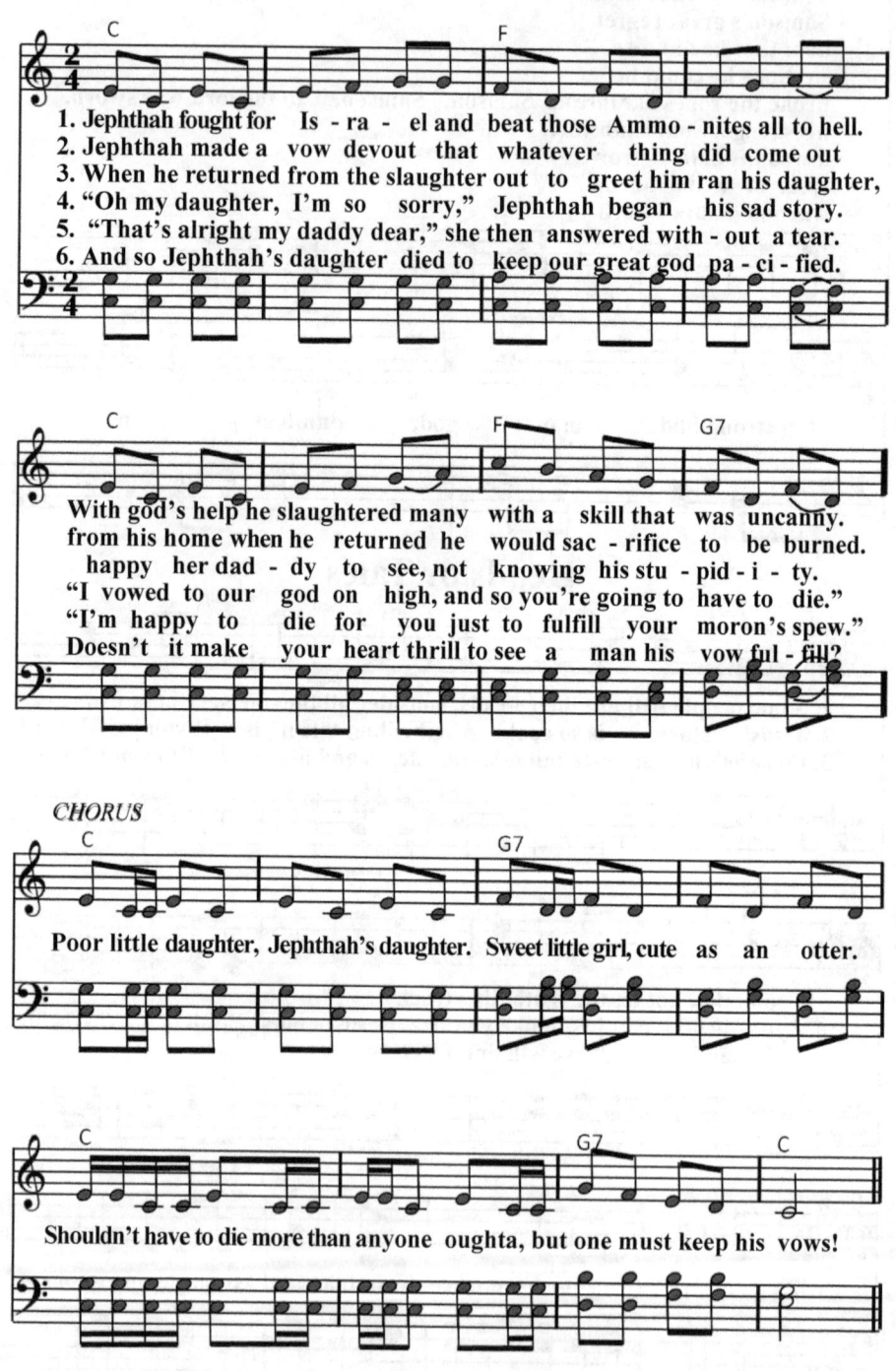

# Foreskins for the King!

*Wherefore David arose and went, he and his men, and slew of the Philistines two hundred men; and David brought their foreskins, and they gave them in full tale to the king, that he might be the king's son in law. -- 1 Samuel 18:27*

1. David loved old King Saul's daughter and she loved him too. But before they could be wed Saul made him pay his due. One hundred Philistine foreskins David would have to pay. Then our warrior so mighty could have his wedding day.
2. So a hundred Philistines he killed with valor fair. Eagerly cut off those skins with love and tender care. When David found it so much fun he killed a hundred more to ensure that old King Saul would his son-in-law a-dore.
3. King Saul gave his daughter then to David as his wife, and he welcomed him to come en-joy the royal life, so glad to have a son-in-law with such great skill to kill, and with those be-loved foreskins his love chest he did fill.

CHORUS
Foreskins for the king! Foreskins for the king! He loves them more than anything. Foreskins for the king!

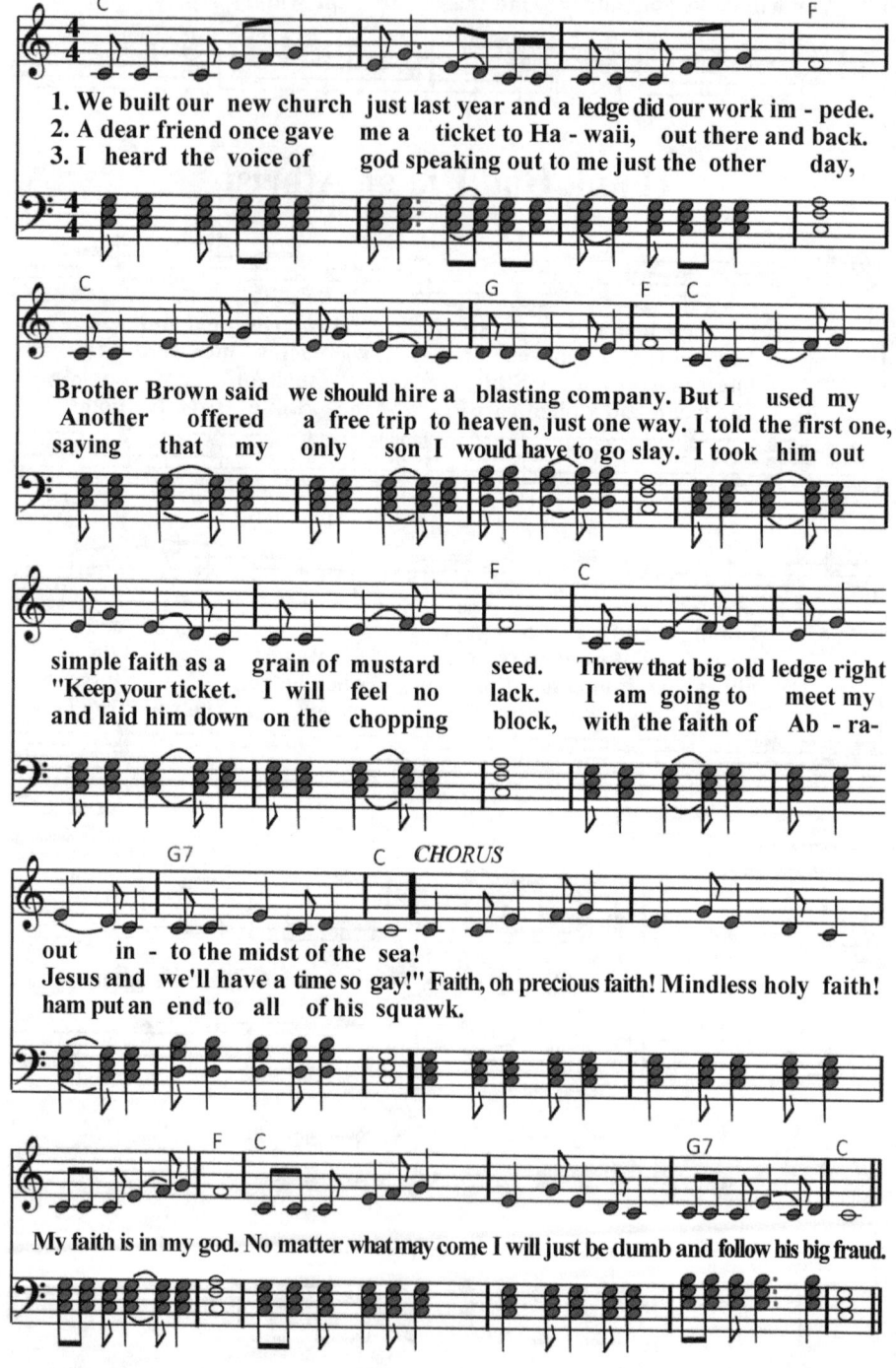

# Because You Don't Believe

*Fear him, which after he hath killed hath power to cast into hell. -- Luke 12:5*

1. My son was such a naughty boy it led me to des-pair, so I killed myself to show how much I care. Then when I came to life he thought it was some kind of trick, so I sent him to hell forever, the little prick!

2. My daughter would not do what's right. She loved to live in sin. Yes, she disobeyed me day out and day in. Yes, even when I'd smite her down my love she just de-nied. Maybe she'll admit it when in hell her ass is fried.

3. My grandchildren I know not well, but they must, too, be bad, since their folks don't even respect their granddad. Besides, I hold the children guilty for their parents' deeds. With my love I'll burn them until their cute eyeballs bleed.

CHORUS

Because you don't be-lieve me down to hell you will go. That is how my love to you I show. I told you a nice story and put on a splendid show. You won't believe so down to hell you go.

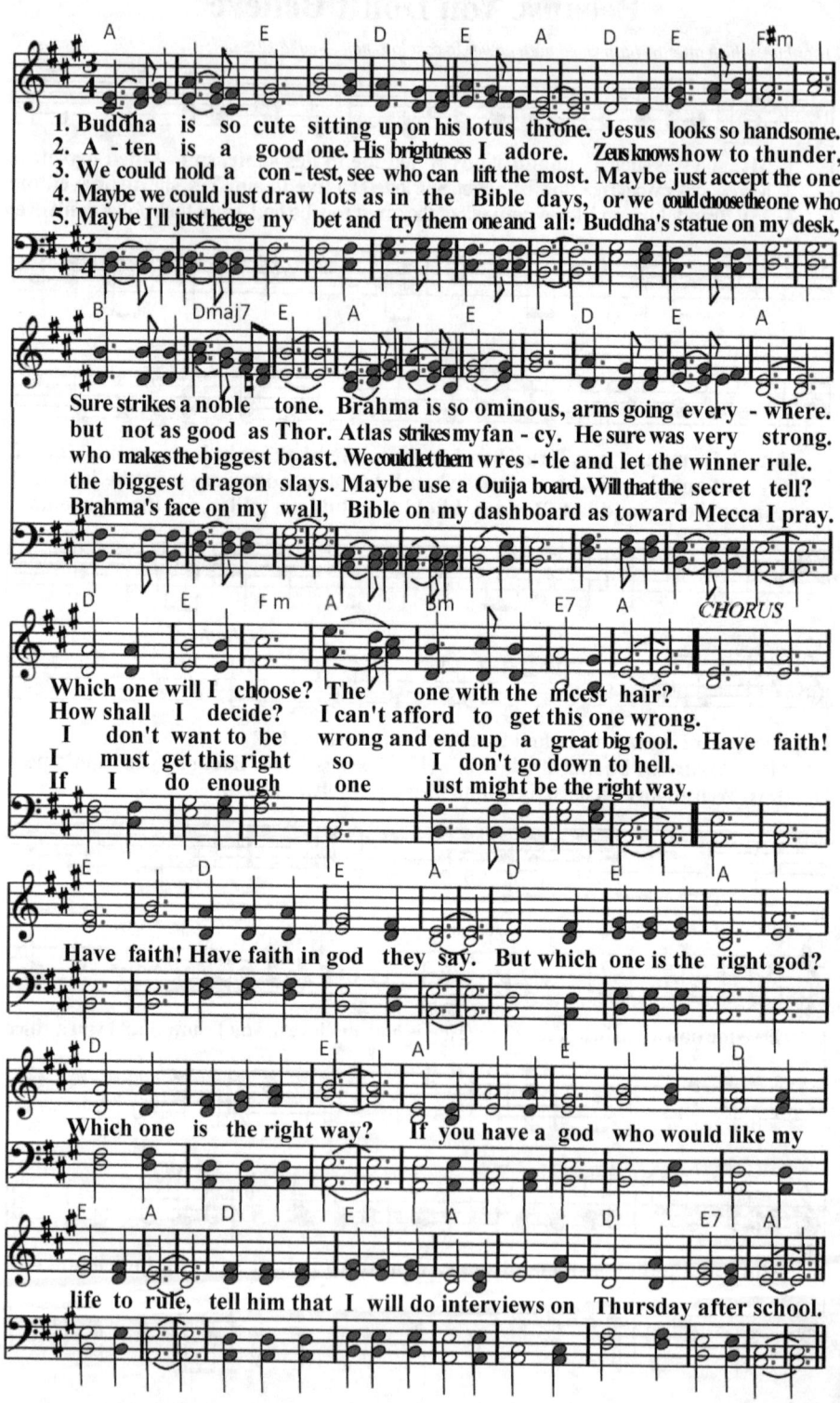

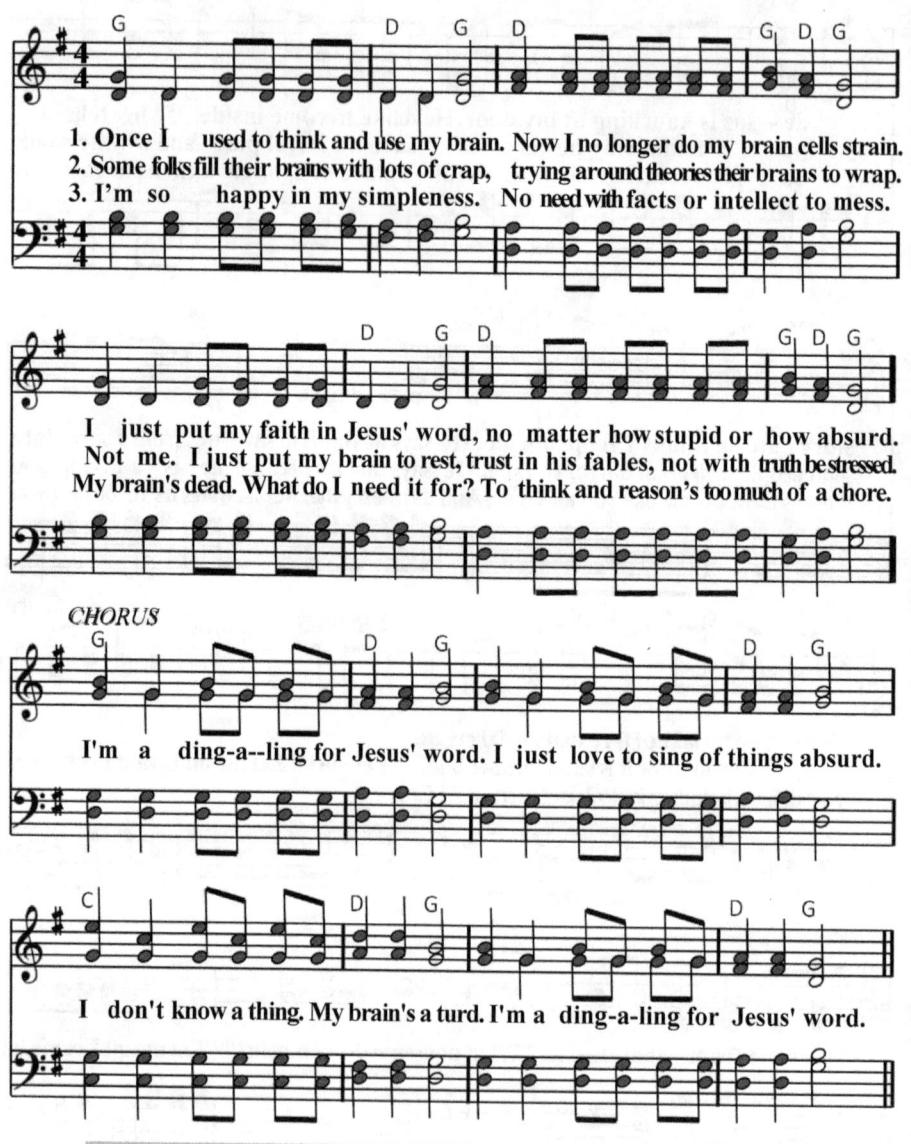

# Ladies Don't You Behave Bad

*...and if thou be defiled, and some man have lain with thee beside thine husband:...this water that causeth the curse shall go into thy bowels, to make thy belly to swell, and thy thigh to rot. -- Number 5:20-22*

The men of Israel were getting out of sorts. They were getting jealous of their female cohorts. They worried that their women were falling prey to vice, and in this way was being spoiled their favorite merchandise.

Well, Moses gave an answer, with god's word so sound. Women would not get a-way with screwing around. They'd drink a vile solution made from dirt off the ground. Using such refined methods, yes, the truth would sure be found.

If you are innocent, oh, so the theory goes, this poison won't hurt you. Safely it through you flows. But if you have been sleeping a-round with other men your thighs will rot, your belly swell and you'll be one sad hen!

So drink this awful mix of water mixed with dirt. If you have not cheated you surely won't be hurt. We'll just make you go through this horrid travesty, oh, whenever your husband feels those pangs of jealousy.

And if you do suspect your husband's been untrue do not try to get him to drink that awful brew. We don't test men to see if they have yielded to vice. We only check the women to protect men's merchandise.

**CHORUS**
Ladies don't you behave bad. You will make your husbands mad. Your thighs will rot, your bellies swell. Then you'll look like hell!

## Heavenly Bliss

*And God shall wipe away all tears from their eyes; and there shall be no more death, neither sorrow, nor crying. -- Revelation 21:14*

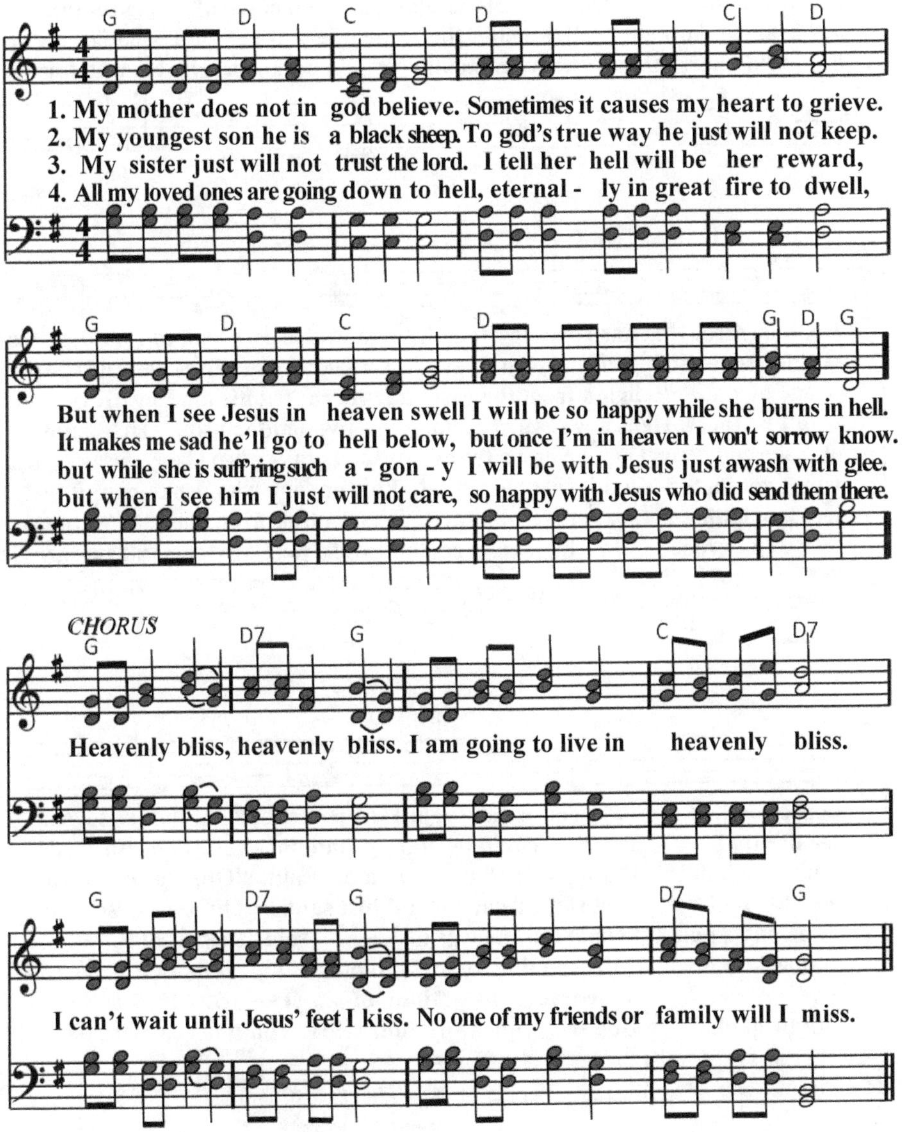

1. My mother does not in god believe. Sometimes it causes my heart to grieve.
2. My youngest son he is a black sheep. To god's true way he just will not keep.
3. My sister just will not trust the lord. I tell her hell will be her reward,
4. All my loved ones are going down to hell, eternal-ly in great fire to dwell,

But when I see Jesus in heaven swell I will be so happy while she burns in hell.
It makes me sad he'll go to hell below, but once I'm in heaven I won't sorrow know.
but while she is suff'ring such a-gon-y I will be with Jesus just awash with glee.
but when I see him I just will not care, so happy with Jesus who did send them there.

**CHORUS**
Heavenly bliss, heavenly bliss. I am going to live in heavenly bliss.
I can't wait until Jesus' feet I kiss. No one of my friends or family will I miss.

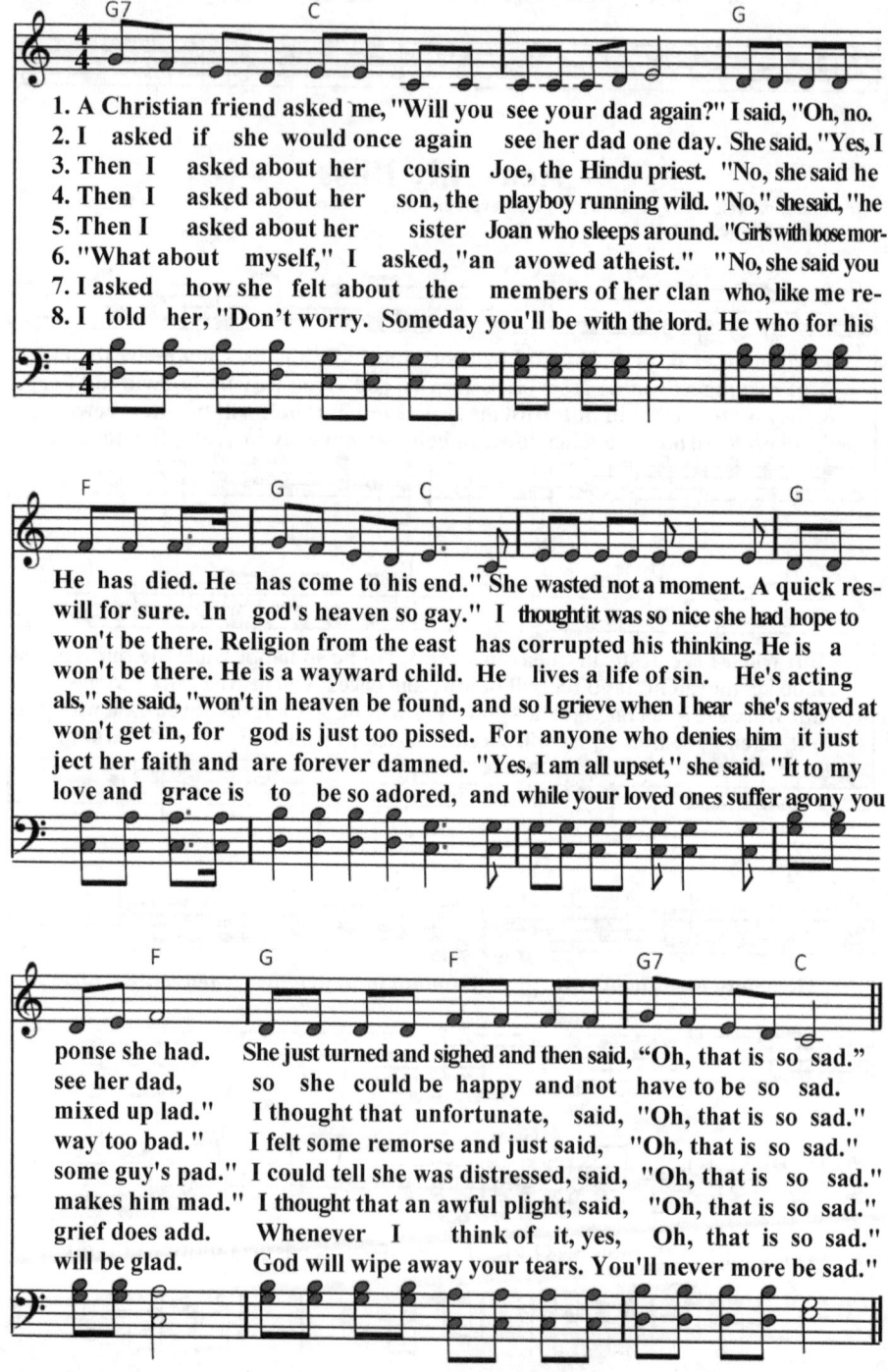

# Fossils Not a Few

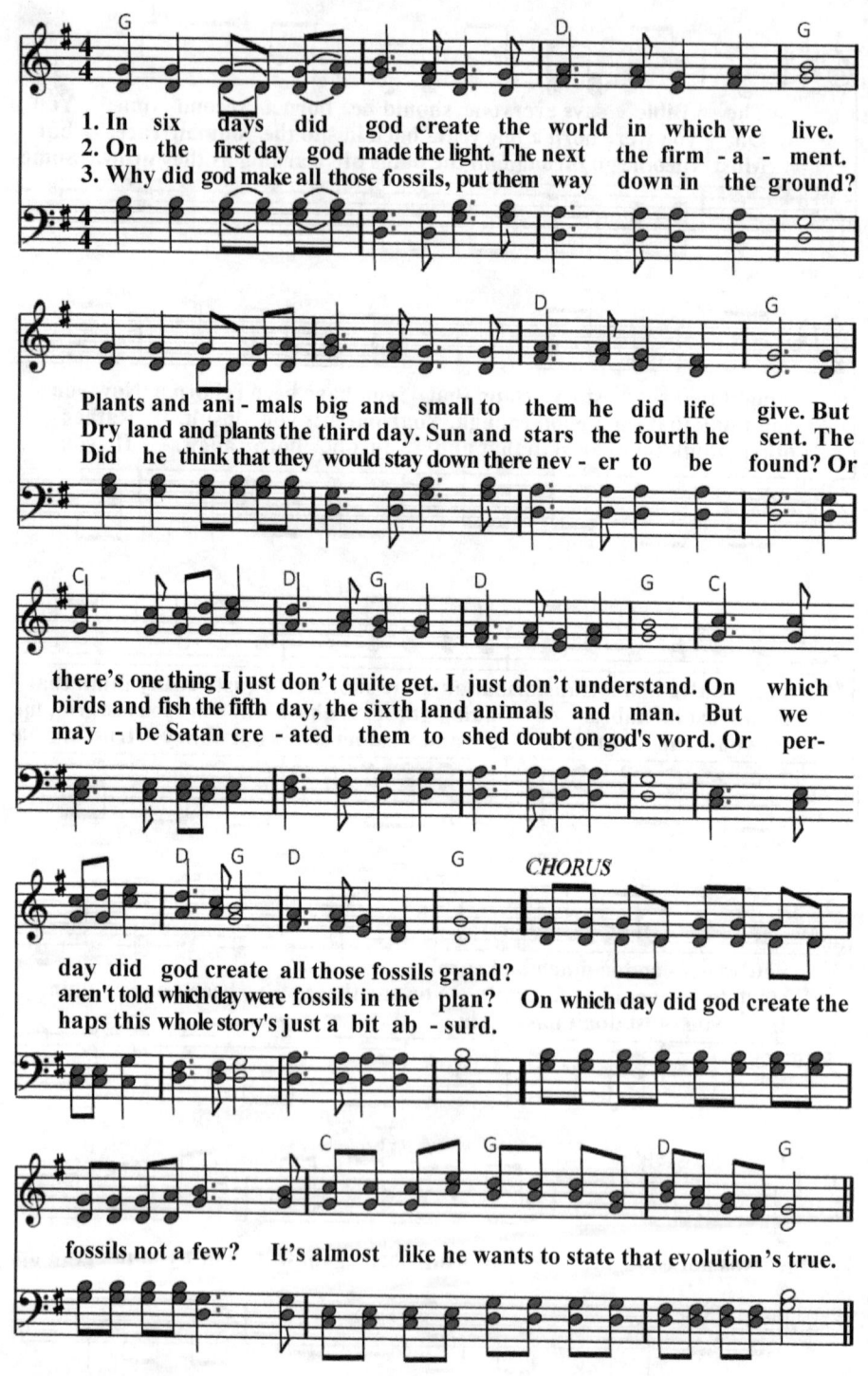

1. In six days did god create the world in which we live.
Plants and animals big and small to them he did life give. But there's one thing I just don't quite get. I just don't understand. On which day did god create all those fossils grand?

2. On the first day god made the light. The next the firmament.
Dry land and plants the third day. Sun and stars the fourth he sent. The birds and fish the fifth day, the sixth land animals and man. But we aren't told which day were fossils in the plan?

3. Why did god make all those fossils, put them way down in the ground?
Did he think that they would stay down there never to be found? Or maybe Satan created them to shed doubt on god's word. Or perhaps this whole story's just a bit absurd.

CHORUS
On which day did god create the fossils not a few? It's almost like he wants to state that evolution's true.

# We Call It the Dark Ages

1. In medieval times interest in science waned. In learning how things worked so little was attained. The church of god, though, it was held in high esteem. The pope's word was in-fal-li-ble. Yes, it was quite a scheme.

2. Greeks had some ideas of how the world might work. You might have thought that from them more ideas would perk. The church of god though, it allowed no heresy. Yes, anything that challenged it was godless blasphemy.

3. The church had the answers. Do not further look. For everything you need comes out of god's great book. Don't bother to think or consider something new. If you try to think for yourself the day you'll surely rue.

CHORUS

There was a time when religion reigned, we learn from history's pages. The church preeminence attained. We call it the Dark Ages.

# We Have a God Who Lives Forever

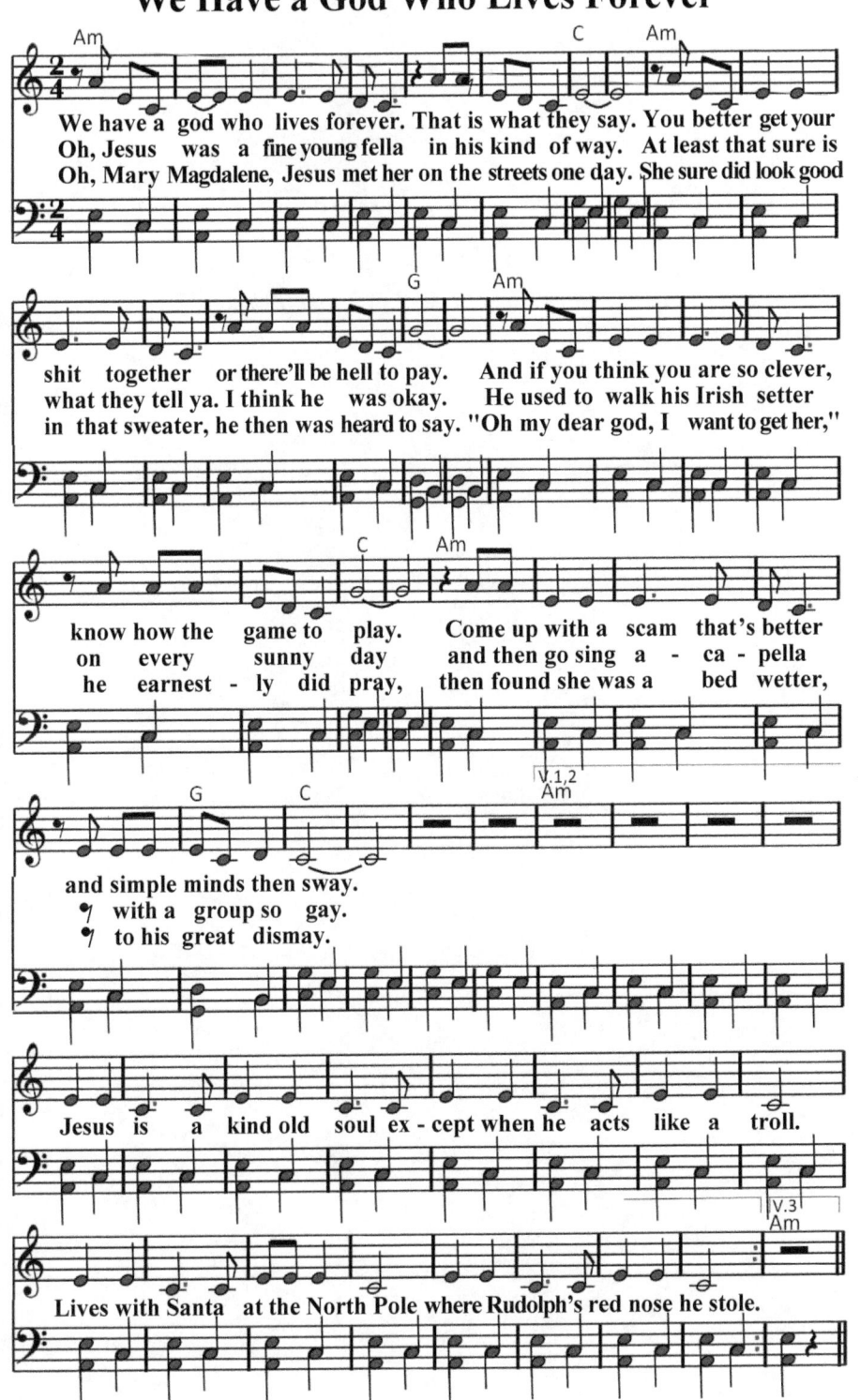

# Index of Titles

Titles that are unchanged are listed in normal font, as are the original titles for songs whose titles have been changed. My titles are in *italics*.

A Child of the King ........................ 106
*A Lot of Crock* .............................. 102
A Mighty Fortress Is Our God ......... 84
*A Might Tortoise Is Our God* ........... 84
*A Missionary Cry* ............................ 36
*A Missionary Cry* ............................ 47
*A New Game So Sorry* ................... 96
A New Name In Glory ..................... 96
A Shelter in the Time of Storm ....... 87
*A Wild, Snotty Thing* .................... 106
Abide With Me ................................ 63
All For Jesus ................................. 108
All Hail the Power of Jesus Name ... 88
*All Stale and Sour Is Jesus' Name* ... 88
All the Way My Savior Leads Me .. 125
Almost Persuaded ........................... 70
Amazing Grace ............................... 16
Angels From the Realms of Glory . 132
Anywhere With Jesus ...................... 25
Are You Washed in the Blood .......... 2
Are You Washed in the Blood ........ 55
*Arise, My Pole, Arise* .................... 124
Arise, My Soul, Arise .................... 124
At Calvary ....................................... 53
At the Cross .................................... 99
*At the Cross I'll Abide* .................... 73
*Barest Lord Jesus* ........................... 90
Battle Hymn of the Republic .......... 14
Be Thou My Vision ....................... 114
*Because You Don't Believe* ........... 157
Beneath the Cross of Jesus ............. 44
*Beneath the Cross of the Serpent* ... 44
*Big Brouhaha, What Behavior!* ...... 89
*Blast This Shame* ........................... 70
Blessed Assurance ........................ 103
Blessed Quietness ......................... 113
Blest Be the Tie That Binds ............. 76
*Blunder-Filled Words of Lies* .......... 60
Breathe On Me, Breath of God ...... 85
Bringing in the Sheaves .................. 64
*Broccoli and Tender Peas* ................ 2

Calling Today ................................. 54
*Can I Go Play, Lord* ........................ 74
Christ Arose .................................... 77
Christ Arose .................................... 98
*Christ In Me* ................................. 113
Christ Is Coming ............................. 29
*Christ the Lord, He Isn't Too Gay* . 124
Christ the Lord Is Risen Today ..... 124
*Christly Fleas!* .............................. 113
Come and Dine ............................ 102
*Come Hide With Me* ...................... 63
*Come Jive Us Again* ..................... 101
Come, Thou Almighty King ........... 88
Come, Thou Fount of Every Bless 123
Come, Thou Long-Expected Jesus 111
*Come, Thou Mount of Shit Distre* 123
Constantly Abiding ......................... 26
*Constantly He's Hiding* .................. 26
*Count Me* ..................................... 120
Count Your Blessings ..................... 57
*Count Your Dressings* .................... 57
*Crave for the Blood* ....................... 75
*Crock of Ages* .............................. 102
*Cross of Christ, Lead Onward* ........ 44
Crown Him With Many Crowns ..... 72
*Cussed Insurance* ......................... 103
*Dancing, Dancing* ............................ 6
Deck the Halls .............................. 131
Deeper and Deeper ........................ 96
*Depraved, Depraved* .................... 107
*Dinosaurs, Oh Dinosaurs* ............. 167
*Don't Rest Ye Weary Gentlemen* . 130
*Don't Spill the Seed* ..................... 141
*Don't Tease the Bald Man* ............ 154
*Draw Me Naked* ............................ 37
Draw Me Nearer ............................. 37
*Eat Your Squash and Your Spuds* ..... 2
*Face Disgrace* .............................. 105
Face to Face ................................. 105
Fairest Lord Jesus ........................... 90
*Faith Is the Trickery* ...................... 67

| | |
|---|---|
| Faith is the Victory | 67 |
| Faith of Our Fathers | 120 |
| Faith, Oh Precious Faith | 156 |
| Fall for Jesus | 108 |
| Fill Me Now | 31 |
| Fill My Cow | 31 |
| Fire Hound | 17 |
| Foreskins for the King! | 153 |
| Fossils Not a Few | 166 |
| Glorious Things of Thee Are Spoke | 78 |
| Glory Be to Him Who Loved Us | 67 |
| Glory To His Name | 33 |
| Go Down, Moses | 21 |
| Go Tell It On the Mountain | 135 |
| Go Ye Into All the World | 66 |
| God Is a Snare to You | 50 |
| God Leads His Dear Children Along | 84 |
| God Leads His Queer Children All | 84 |
| God of War, Lead Onward | 44 |
| God Moves in a Mysterious Way | 50 |
| God Rest Ye Merry Gentlemen | 130 |
| God Will Take Care of You | 32 |
| God Will Take Care of You | 50 |
| God's Unaware of You | 32 |
| Grace Greater Than Our Sin | 22 |
| Grace That Killed Others for David | 22 |
| Greensleeves | 129 |
| Guide Me Not, Thou Great Big Jok | 50 |
| Guide Me, O Thou Great Jehovah | 50 |
| Ha, Ha, Pharaoh! | 145 |
| Hallelujah, What a Savior | 89 |
| Harden Pharaoh's Heart | 21 |
| Hark! The Herald Angels Sing | 136 |
| Hark! The Herald Angels Stink | 136 |
| Have Thine Own Way, Lord | 74 |
| Haze Him! Haze Him! | 112 |
| He Breedeth Fleas, Oh, Wretched | 32 |
| He Is Able To Deliver Thee | 83 |
| He Is Saber-Toothed and Slithery | 83 |
| He Is So Willing | 46 |
| He Keeps Me Singing | 7 |
| He Leadeth Me, O Blessed Thoug | 32 |
| He Keeps Me Singing | 62 |
| He Played Hell With My Soul | 30 |
| He Was Not Willing | 46 |
| Heads or Tales | 151 |
| Heavenly Bliss | 163 |
| Heavenly Sunlight | 34 |
| Helter-Skelter in a Slimy Moor | 87 |
| He's Just Not the Flip-Flopping Kin | 55 |
| Hiding From Thee | 90 |
| Hiding In Thee | 90 |
| Higher Ground | 17 |
| Higher It Grows | 104 |
| Himself | 61 |
| His Eye Is On the Sparrow | 46 |
| His Way With Thee | 24 |
| Holey, Holey, Holey | 106 |
| Holy Bible, Book Divine | 65 |
| Holy, Holy, Holy | 106 |
| Hound Him With Many Clowns | 72 |
| How Firm a Foundation | 77 |
| How Gory, Gory Is My Lord | 82 |
| How Marvelous, How Wonderful | 62 |
| How Marvelous, How Wonderful | 118 |
| How Obscene | 58 |
| How Odd Is the Story | 118 |
| I Am a Deadbeat Dad | 85 |
| I Am Cross, Fit to Be Tied | 73 |
| I Am Wary Just to Walk With Him | 58 |
| I Cower In Prayer | 30 |
| I Have Decided to Follow Jesus | 95 |
| I Have Decided to Swallow Jesus | 95 |
| I Heard the Voice of Jesus Say | 78 |
| I Know That My C-Cleaner Lives | 71 |
| I Know That My Redeemer Lives | 71 |
| I Know Whom I Have Believed | 120 |
| I Love to Tell a Story | 16 |
| I Love to Tell the Story | 16 |
| I Love to Tell the Story | 95 |
| I Need Pee Every Hour | 10 |
| I Need Thee Every Hour | 10 |
| I Saw the Cross of Jesus | 91 |
| I Schemed. How I Love to Proclaim | 97 |
| I Will Sing the Wondrous Story | 68 |
| I Would Be Like Jesus | 54 |
| I'll Go Where You Want Me to Go | 97 |
| I'll Troll Where You Want Me to T | 97 |
| I'm a Ding-A-Ling for Jesus' Word | 160 |
| I'm Redeemed | 58 |
| Imaginary Friend Is Jesus | 51 |
| In the Garden | 55 |

# Index

In the Hour of Trial ........................ 53
In the Sweet By and By ................ 110
*Intelligent Design* ........................ 139
*Is It the Clowning Day?* ................ 72
Is It the Crowning Day? ................. 72
Is My Name Written There? .......... 28
*Is Thy Heart Right in Thy Bod* ....... 10
Is Thy Heart Right With God .......... 10
It is Glory Just to Walk With Him ... 58
It Is Well With My Soul ................. 30
*I've Won the Disgrace of Jesus* ...... 25
*Jephthah's Daughter* ................... 152
*Jesus Giveth Us the Fib Story* ......... 99
Jesus Giveth Us the Victory ........... 99
Jesus, I Come ................................ 109
Jesus Is All the World to Me ......... 92
*Jesus Is Like a Squirrel to Me* ........ 92
*Jesus, Jesus, Jesus* ........................ 62
Jesus, Lover of My Soul ................. 87
*Jesus Loves Even Fleas* ................. 26
Jesus Loves Even Me ..................... 26
Jesus Loves Me, This I Know ......... 65
Jesus Loves the Little Children ...... 49
Jesus Paid It All .............................. 9
Jesus Only ..................................... 91
*Jesus Phony* .................................. 91
*Jesus Played Baseball* .................... 9
Jesus Saves ................................... 27
*Jesus Shaves* ................................ 27
*Jesus, You Are Such a Troll* ........... 87
Joy to the World ......................... 132
Joy Unspeakable ......................... 101
Just As I Am ................................ 122
*Just Look at Him Sway Pretty* ....... 24
Keep In Touch With Jesus ............. 52
Korah, Korah ............................... 148
*Ladies Don't You Behave Bad* ..... 161
Launch Out ................................... 20
Lead On, O King Eternal ............... 85
Lead On, O King Eternal ............... 86
*Lead On, Oh King Infernal* ........... 86
Leaning On the Everlasting Arms ... 8
Leaning On the Everlasting Arms .. 62
*Leaning On the Never Lasting Arm* 62
*Let Me In!* ................................. 159
Let My People Go ......................... 21
Let Us Break Bread Together on .... 38
*Let Us Break Heads Together, If* ..... 38
Like a River Glorious ..................... 98
*Listen Heaven, and I Will Speak* ... 131
Living In Sunlight .......................... 34
Living In the Glory ........................ 82
Lo, He Comes With Clouds Descen 26
*Lo, He Drums With Clowns Unend* . 26
Lord, I Want to Be a Christian ...... 121
Lord, I'm Coming Home ................ 34
Love Divine, All Loves Excelling .... 123
*Love Divine, Your Butt Is Smelling* 123
Love Found a Way ........................ 71
Loyalty to Christ .............................. 3
*Make Slime, Roly-Polies* ............... 89
Moment By Moment ..................... 57
More Holiness Give Me ............... 119
*More Oiliness Give Me* ............... 119
*Music, Music, Music* ...................... 7
Must Jesus Bear the Cross Alone ... 90
*Must Jesus Swear and Cuss Alone* .. 90
My Anchor Holds ........................... 12
My Anchor Holds ........................... 34
*My Cheeses, I Love Thee* ................ 3
*My Deodorant Holds* ................... 12
*My Faith and Gullibility* ............... 105
My Faith Looks Up to Thee ......... 105
My Jesus, I Love Thee ..................... 3
My Redeemer ............................... 54
Near the Cross .............................. 59
*Near to the Fart of God* ................ 85
Near to the Heart of God .............. 85
Nearer, My God, To Thee .............. 48
Nearer, Still Nearer ....................... 48
*No Longer Will I Squander* ........... 69
Nor Silver Nor Gold ....................... 30
Not I, But Christ .............................. 6
Nothing Between ........................ 121
Nothing But the Blood ................ 100
*Nothing But the Crud* ................ 100
Now I'm Coming Home ................. 34
*Now Spank We All Our God* ......... 82
Now Thank We All Our God ......... 82
O Come All Ye Faithful ................ 135
O For a Thousand Tongues to Sing 73
O God, Our Help in Ages Past ..... 125

O, Holy Night .................................. 133
O Love That Wilt Not Let Me Go .... 64
O That Will Be Glory ..................... 107
O Worship the King ........................ 39
Oh, Come All Ye Mindless ............ 135
Oh, Drug That Wilt Not Let Me Go 64
Oh, Earth Ship Please Swing .......... 39
Oh, For a Thousand Stunts to Spri .. 73
Oh, God Has Felt the Sage's Ass ... 125
Oh, Happy Day ............................. 109
Oh, Holy Cripe! ............................. 133
Oh, How I Love Jesus ..................... 93
Oh, Job, He Is My Man ................... 20
Oh, Little Town of Bethlehem ...... 133
Oh, That Is So Sad ........................ 164
Oh, Will You Feel Sorry? ............... 107
Oily Peas for Christ .......................... 3
Old Time Power .............................. 11
On Jordan's Stormy Banks I Stand . 43
Once ............................................... 61
Once for All .................................... 35
One Day! ........................................ 92
Only Believe ................................... 59
Only Trust Him ............................... 96
Only Trust Him ............................... 98
Onward Christian Soldiers ............. 45
Open My Eyes That I May See ..... 105
Paddling My Kayak on the Great Bl . 8
Pass Me Not ................................... 53
Pass the Pot ................................... 53
Peace, Perfect Peace ...................... 35
Peace, Perfect Piece ..................... 111
Peas, Perfect Peas ........................ 111
Pesky the Guy That Whines ........... 76
Piece, Perfect Piece ....................... 35
Please Spare Me, Breath of God .... 85
Plunder His Things ......................... 74
Pokey Is His Name .......................... 33
Pot Pies for Christ ............................ 6
Praise God From Whom All Smitin . 32
Praise God From Whom All Blessi .. 32
Praise Him, Praise Him ..................... 6
Praise Him, Praise Him ................. 112
Precious Name ............................... 70
Queer the Cross ............................. 59
Queerer, My God, Art Thee ........... 48

Queerer, Still Queerer .................... 48
Read the Bible Every Day .............. 65
Rescue the Perishing ..................... 68
Revive Us Again ........................... 101
Rex, Rex the Dinosaur ................. 144
Rock of Ages ................................ 102
Rusting Jesus ................................. 73
Safe From the Harms of Jesus ....... 56
Safe In the Arms of Jesus .............. 56
Samson, Samson .......................... 150
Saved By the Blood ....................... 75
Saved, Saved ............................... 107
Saved, Saved, Saved ...................... 11
Saved, Saved, Saved .................... 122
Saving and Serving .......................... 8
Savior, Like a Shepherd Lead Us .... 88
Scour Out the Crud ....................... 69
Seek Out New Temptations ........ 112
Send Refreshing ............................ 20
Send the Fire ................................. 20
Send the Fire ................................. 22
Send the Light ............................... 22
Shall We Blather at the River ...... 110
Shall We Gather at the River ...... 110
Shun That Unsightly Thing ............ 88
Shut Up Inside the Church! ......... 149
Silent Night ................................. 135
Since I Have Been Deceived .......... 61
Since I Have Been Redeemed ......... 7
Since I Have Been Redeemed ....... 61
Since I Have Eaten Ice Cream ......... 7
Since Jesus Came Into My Heart .. 104
Since the Bullshit of His Love Th ... 103
Since the Fullness of His Love Ca . 103
Singing in the Eaves ...................... 64
Six Inches a Minute ..................... 138
Sneeze! Sneeze! Sneeze! .............. 11
Softly and Tenderly ......................... 2
Solar Power ................................... 11
Soldiers of Christ, Arise! ................ 15
Soldiers of Christ, Arise! .............. 119
Soldiers of Christ, Surprise! ......... 119
Soldiers of Peace, Arise! ................ 15
Somebody's Knocking at Your Door 55
Son of a Troll ................................. 86
Sorry Be to Him Who Trusts Us ..... 67

| | |
|---|---|
| Soy to the World ........................... 132 | The Yellow Stream ........................ 76 |
| Speed the Light ............................. 70 | There is a Fountain Filled With Blo 42 |
| Stand Up for Jesus ......................... 15 | There is Flour in the Bread .............. 4 |
| Stand Up for Jesus ......................... 91 | There is Power in the Blood ............ 4 |
| Stand Up for Peace ........................ 15 | There is Power in the Blood .......... 69 |
| Standing on the Promises ............. 60 | There Shall Be Plowers Undressing 17 |
| Step By Step ................................... 10 | There Shall Be Showers of Blessing 17 |
| Step By Step ................................... 27 | There's a Snideness in God's Mercy 33 |
| Still Sweeter Every Day ................... 94 | There's a Wideness in God's Mercy 33 |
| Stop That Tower ........................... 142 | They Arose ..................................... 77 |
| Stranded on the Promises ............. 60 | They're Jezzing Up Their Brooms ... 36 |
| Sun of My Soul ............................... 86 | They're Passing To Their Doom ..... 47 |
| Sunshine in the Soul .................... 124 | Thrust All the Way ....................... 122 |
| Sunshine on My Pole ................... 124 | Thunder-Filled, Blunder-Filled Jesu 56 |
| Sweet Hour of Prayer .................... 30 | Thy Word Is Like a Garden, Lord ... 65 |
| Swing Low, Sweet Chariot ........... 110 | 'Tis Burning in My Soul .................. 23 |
| Take My Life and Let It Be ............. 31 | 'Tis Burning in Their Streets .......... 23 |
| Take My Wife and Let Me Be ......... 31 | 'Tis So Sweet to Eat the Chocolate... 4 |
| Take Time to Be Holy ..................... 89 | 'Tis So Sweet to Trust In Jesus ......... 4 |
| Telepathic Messages ................... 162 | 'Tis So Sweet to Trust In Jesus ..... 108 |
| Tell Me a Big, Tall Story ................ 100 | To Be Like Jesus ............................. 76 |
| Tell Me the Old, Old Story ........... 100 | To God Be the Glory .................... 118 |
| Tell Me the Story of Jacob ............. 24 | To Pee Like Jesus ........................... 76 |
| Tell Me the Story of Jesus ............. 24 | To Pray to the Cross Say "Om" ...... 78 |
| Thank God I'm an Atheist ............ 155 | To the Regions Beyond ................. 66 |
| The Calvary ..................................... 53 | Torment By Torment ..................... 57 |
| The Church's Inundation ............... 74 | Trust and Obey ............................ 122 |
| The Church's One Foundation ....... 74 | Trusting Jesus ................................ 73 |
| The Conflict of the Ages ................ 13 | 'Twas a Bad Day When Jesus Foun 28 |
| The Conflict of the Ages ................ 37 | 'Twas a Glad Day When Jesus Fou. 28 |
| The Conflicts of the Ages ............. 13 | Under His Wings ........................... 74 |
| The Conflicts of the Pages ............. 37 | Underwear for Jesus ..................... 25 |
| The Cleansing Wave ....................... 76 | We Call It the Dark Ages .............. 168 |
| The Comforter Has Come .............. 83 | We Have a God Who Lives Forev. 169 |
| The Dumb Flirter Has Come ........... 83 | We Three Kings of Orient Are ...... 134 |
| The Fire is Burning ......................... 23 | We're Marching to Zion ................. 13 |
| The First "Oh, Hell!" ..................... 128 | We're Marching to Zion ................. 63 |
| The First Noel .............................. 128 | We're Starching Our Nylons .......... 63 |
| The God of Abraham Praise .......... 45 | We're Working Together ............... 13 |
| The Lily of the Valley ..................... 52 | Were You There ........................... 106 |
| The Lord Hears My F-Word ........... 79 | We've a Story to Tell to the Nation 66 |
| The Lord Is My Shepherd ............... 79 | What a Fib Uproarious .................. 98 |
| The Solid Rock ............................. 102 | What A Friend We Have In Jesus ..... 9 |
| The Twelve Days of Christmas ..... 132 | What a Friend We Have in Jesus ... 51 |
| The Twelve Weeks of Sunday Sco. 132 | What a Hoax! ................................. 98 |
| The Way of the Cross Leads Home. 78 | What A Joy There Is in Hiking ......... 9 |

| | |
|---|---|
| *What a Wonderful Flavor* ............... 75 | *Wiley Schemer* .................................. 54 |
| What a Wonderful Savior ............... 75 | *Will You Eat Pie In the Sky?* .......... 110 |
| What Child Is This? ....................... 129 | Wonderful Grace of Jesus ................. 5 |
| What If It Were Today? .................. 29 | Wonderful Grace of Jesus ............... 25 |
| *What Squirmy Gyrations* ............... 77 | *Wonderful, Nitwitted Friend* .......... 94 |
| *When I Purvey the Blunderous Cro* 68 | *Wonderful Taste of Peanuts* ............ 5 |
| When I Survey the Wondrous Cros 68 | Wonderful, Unfailing Friend .......... 94 |
| When I See the Blood ..................... 43 | Wonderful, Wonderful Jesus ......... 56 |
| When Morning Gilds the Skies ...... 86 | Wonderful Words of Life ............... 60 |
| *When Mourning Fills the Skies* ...... 86 | *Yay, Yay, Levites!* ......................... 146 |
| When the Roll Is Called Up Yonder.. 5 | Ye Must Be Born Again ................ 116 |
| When the Roll Is Called Up Yonder 69 | *Ye Must Read Porn Again* ............ 116 |
| *When the Rolls Are Served With B* ... 5 | *Yesterday They Weren't So Clever* . 36 |
| When the Saints Go Marching In ... 39 | Yesterday, Today, Forever ............. 36 |
| When We All Get to Heaven ........ 109 | *Yield Not Perspiration* .................... 12 |
| Where He Lead Me ...................... 114 | Yield Not to Temptation ................ 12 |
| Where Jesus Is "Tis Heaven There . 89 | Yield Not to Temptation .............. 112 |
| *Where Jesus Is "Tis Quite a Scare* .. 89 | You May Have the Joy-Bells ......... 115 |
| *Which One Will I Choose?* ............ 158 | *You May Have the Joy-Smells* ...... 115 |
| While Shepherds Watched Their . 131 | *You Say That You've Been Born A* 165 |
| Whiter Than Snow ....................... 104 | *You Screwed My Vision* ................ 114 |
| Whosoever Will ............................. 59 | *You're Gonna Need a Bigger Boat* 140 |

CPSIA information can be obtained
at www.ICGtesting.com
Printed in the USA
FFHW01n0933170818
47710389-51366FF